SAILBOAT ELECTRICS SIMPLIFIED

DON CASEY

THE INTERNATIONAL MARINE SAILBOAT LIBRARY

SAILBOAT ELECTRICS SIMPLIFIED

DON CASEY

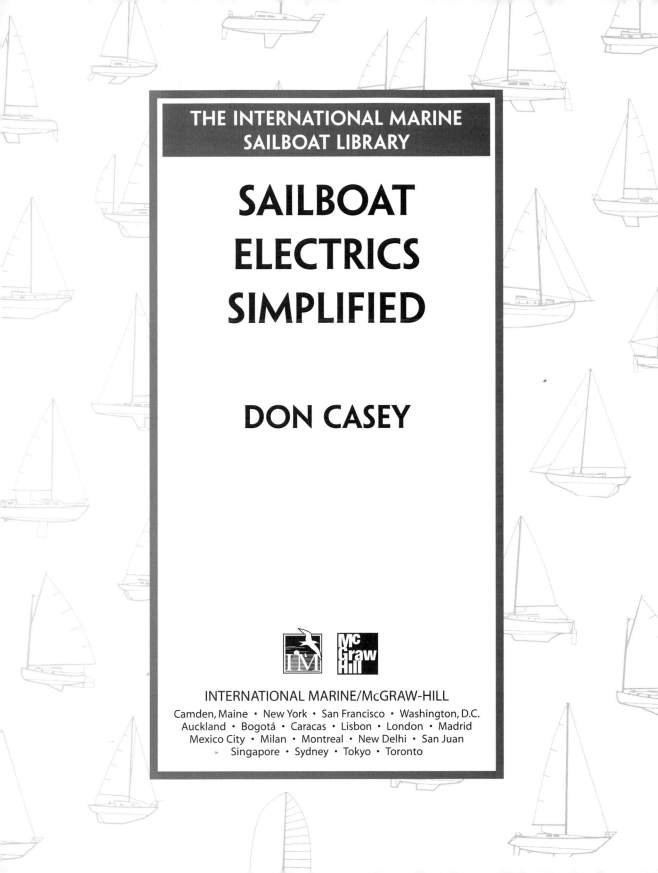

INTERNATIONAL MARINE/McGRAW-HILL

Camden, Maine • New York • San Francisco • Washington, D.C.
Auckland • Bogotá • Caracas • Lisbon • London • Madrid
Mexico City • Milan • Montreal • New Delhi • San Juan
Singapore • Sydney • Tokyo • Toronto

International Marine

A Division of The **McGraw·Hill** *Companies*

10   9   8   7   6   5   4

Library of Congress Cataloging-in-Publication Data
Casey, Don.
    Sailboat electrics simplified / Don Casey.
            p.   cm.
        Includes index.
        ISBN 0-07-036649-7 (alk. paper)
        1. Boats and boating—Electric equipment—Amateurs' manuals.
        2. Sailboats—Maintenance and repair—Amateurs' manuals.   I. Title.
    VM325.C37 1999
    623.8'52—dc21   98-53152
                                                              CIP

Questions regarding the content of this book should be addressed to:
    International Marine
    P.O. Box 220
    Camden, ME 04843
    Visit us on the World Wide Web at www.internationalmarine.com

Questions regarding the ordering of this book should be addressed to:
    The McGraw-Hill Companies
    Customer Service Department
    P.O. Box 547
    Blacklick, OH 43004
    Retail customers: 1-800-262-4729
    Bookstores: 1-800-722-4726

This book is printed on 70-pound Citation.

Illustrations by the author, Kim Downing, Jamie Downing, and Jim Sollers
Cover photo by William Thuss
Cover illustrations: Boats by Jim Sollers; electrical drawing by Kim Downing
Printed by R. R. Donnelly, Crawfordsville, IN
Design and layout by Ann Aspell
Production by Shannon Thomas
Project management by Janet Robbins
Edited by Jon Eaton, Mary Sullivan, and D. A. Oliver

Dedicated to Bill Laudeman,
who blazed the trail for this book, and
whose strong convictions about the value
of wiring diagrams were the genesis of
much of Chapter 5

CONTENTS

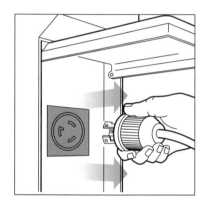

INTRODUCTION

I admire those hard cases who, before setting off around the globe, lever the engine out of the bilge and tilt it over the rail, deep-sixing a whole passel of woes. The time not spent doing maintenance can effectively add weeks to a cruise. Maybe the engineless do miss a few destinations with difficult approaches, but they also avoid languishing in some overdeveloped and under-flushed harbor awaiting the arrival of transmission parts. They never spill fuel, smudge the transom with soot, or besmirch profound silence with the clatter of reciprocating iron. Discarding the engine also rules out mechanical refrigeration, you won't find a watermaker aboard, and the absence of an engine-driven alternator necessarily simplifies the boat's electrical system.

I am personally OK with ice for uncomplicated refrigeration, and to me catching water actually seems preferable to "making" it, but when I contemplate kerosene lighting, the simplicity of "pure" sail loses all appeal. Kerosene illumination bright enough to read by will add at least 20 degrees to the cabin temperature. That may be nice when it is 40°F outside, but when it's 85°F—well, you do the math.

On my boat I want bright and cool electric lights. While that doesn't necessarily require an alternator powered by a 500-pound diesel engine—a couple of solar panels can provide enough electricity for cabin lights—I also want fans. And a radio transmitter. And a good sound system. When the anchorages get deep, I could use the help of an electric windlass. And speaking of hauling, resupplying the cooler with ice gets to be a drag quicker than I like to admit.

This, of course, is how electrical systems on boats evolve. Production sailboats come with a few lights, a freshwater pump, and the expectation that the purchaser will add a depth sounder and a VHF radio. The alternator, the battery, even the wiring are designed for these modest demands. The owner, however, is rarely of a mind with the manufacturer.

Maybe it starts with adding a reading light over a bunk. While a new lamp for home comes with a plug we simply insert into any unoccupied wall outlet, a lamp for the boat brings only a few inches of wire lead. Now what? Far too often the answer is a length of lamp cord twisted to the bare leads on one end and wrapped on the other around the terminal screws of the nearest cabin light.

What is wrong with that? Just about everything.

Adding appliances to your boat's existing electrical system is neither difficult nor complicated, but it is exacting if the modification is to be safe and trouble free. Sometimes sailors use the wrong wire because it is handy, but more often they simply don't know any better. If you're connecting a lamp, what can be wrong with using lamp cord? And if it is adequate for a 100-watt table lamp, how can it be inadequate for a 10-watt reading lamp? Fair questions, both, and their answers are provided in Chapter 4.

Most of us find electricity as incomprehensible as the tax code. Who really understands the basis for subtracting line 8 from line 5, then multiplying by 0.25 to get line 9, "but do not enter more than line 6"? So we pay someone to do our taxes. Or we buy Turbo Tax to tell us—without the bureaucratic doublespeak—exactly what to write on each line of the tax form and not trouble us with the why unless we ask. The underlying concept for this book is much the same—Turbo Wiring, if you will.

The objective of this book is to show you exactly how to service and modify the electrical system on your boat. Assuming that the less theory I throw at you, the happier you're going to be, I have included electrical arcana only where it is absolutely essential. But here's the deal: if I try to keep this dead simple for the masses, the eggheads in the bunch can't take me to task for taking liberties. I'm not teaching electricity here. I'm just trying to show you how to make a safe, durable connection.

OK, that isn't quite all there is to it. The connection I am really trying to help you make is the one between you and the electrical system aboard your boat—figuratively speaking, of course. For example, if you understand amp-hours the way you understand gallons, determining how long your batteries will run all the boat's electrical equipment is as easy as calculating how far you can expect to motor on a tank of fuel.

So when I describe amps in the following pages, it is for practical use, not scientific—something like introducing European tourists to mph. It isn't necessary to know that a mile is 1,609 meters when speedometers, maps, and road signs are all in mph. Likewise, you can read amps directly from a meter and make the necessary correlations without any understanding of the underlying science.

You will find practical information here about batteries—gel cells versus the flooded variety, cranking batteries versus deep cycle. You will learn how to select the "right" wire and how to make "good" connections. You will learn to calculate how quickly your electrical equipment will deplete your batteries, and how to counteract that drain with both traditional and alternative power sources.

Besides a handful of electrical terms, I will expose you to a few symbols that let you "map" your boat's electrical system, taking a lot of guesswork out of troubleshooting. You will see how to isolate problems quickly using a multimeter—where to connect the test probes and exactly what specific readings mean. (An adequate digital multimeter today costs less than this book and every boatowner should have one!)

You will find enough information about marine electronics to let you install new gear, enough about alternating current to avoid or correct the most common shore-power problems, and enough about lightning to let you maximize your level of protection from this unpredictable menace.

So put aside your preconceptions and turn the page. I promise explanations and instructions as uncomplicated as I can make them. There is nothing here that should put you at risk. To the contrary, understanding the wiring on your boat should only make you safer. The only shock you are likely to experience is how easy this stuff really is.

CHAPTER 1
SAFETY FIRST

A lot of people are of the opinion that messing around with electricity is just asking for it. Touch the wrong wire and it's off to Fiddler's Green. Respect for the dangers of electricity is a good thing—not something I want to talk you out of. But the bulk of this book concerns battery-powered electrical systems that operate on what is called *direct current* or DC. DC voltage has to get up around 600 volts to represent a serious shock risk. Working on your boat's 12-volt electrical system has the same shock potential as changing the batteries in a portable lantern—none.

Alternating current (AC) is another matter, whether provided by an outlet on the dock, an onboard generator, or even an inverter. The pulsating nature of AC can interfere with your heart's natural rhythm, and a fatal disruption is possible with as little as 60 volts AC. Since onboard AC circuits carry at least 110 volts, you must take all necessary precautions to make sure you don't accidentally touch the wrong wire. As long as you disconnect the power supply first, it is possible to work on AC circuits in complete safety, but that means *all* power supplies. Keep in mind that an inverter energizes the AC circuits even when the boat is unplugged. If you are at all unsure, leave AC circuits to someone else.

Twelve-volt circuits won't shock you no matter which wires you touch, but that doesn't mean you can dispense with caution. There are other safety issues you should keep in mind.

BATTERY ACID

The liquid (electrolyte) inside a battery is a sulfuric acid solution. Spill it on yourself and it will eat clothes and burn skin. Never peer closely into the cells to check the water level; a popping bubble can spray enough acid in your eyes to cause permanent impairment, even blindness. Wear eye protection when working around batteries. If you do splash battery acid, flush it immediately with freshwater (*not* seawater, which gives off deadly chlorine gas when combined with battery acid). Neutralize the spill with baking soda.

CONTAINMENT

Mount batteries in an acid-proof box. Cracked battery cases are not unknown, and in such an event a box eliminates or minimizes collateral damage. You can purchase polypropylene battery boxes or construct your own using plywood sheathed in fiberglass.

Should a heavy battery come adrift, it can cause serious damage and injury. It is imperative to secure all batteries with strong straps or restraining rods.

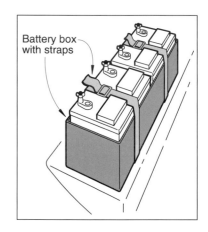

Battery box with straps

SPARK

If you have ever attached jumper cables, you have no doubt seen the sparking potential of a 12-volt battery. Electrical arcs—the basis for arc welding—generate tremendous heat. Accidentally touch a wrench to both terminals of a charged battery and the current will cut a notch in the wrench—and maybe in your hand. Remove all metal jewelry before working on battery connections.

Small wires can also spark, but with much less consequence because the current is limited by wire size and probably a fuse. However, any spark is dangerous in the presence of explosive fumes. Be sure the bilge is clear of propane or gasoline fumes before working on your electrical system.

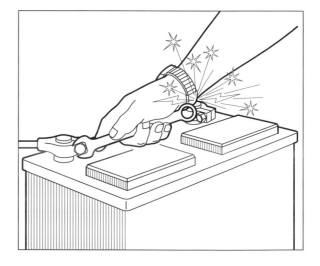

EXPLOSIVE GAS

When charging, batteries produce both hydrogen and oxygen—a volatile cocktail. Both gases are lighter than air, so they don't settle into the bilge, but they can accumulate in the battery compartment. Effective ventilation is a battery-compartment essential.

Never work on the electrical system while the battery is charging. Even if the batteries are well ventilated, the "head" of the cells is full of hydrogen and oxygen.

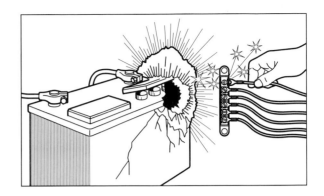

FIRE

Fire is far and away the most common consequence of inadequate or careless wiring. Resistance causes a conductor to get hot—the principle behind the burner coils on an electric range. Wire too small for the job, poor connections, and corrosion can all result in excessive and dangerous resistance. Hot wiring is most dangerous when it is in contact with flammables like paper or cloth, but a hot wire directly igniting polyester resin (fiberglass) is not unknown.

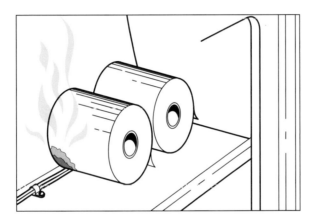

Protect against electrical fire by using large enough wire (tables are provided in Chapter 4). Tin-plated ("tinned") wire is much more corrosion resistant than bare copper. Terminals should likewise be tinned copper, never aluminum. Use only copper or brass washers on screw terminals, not steel or aluminum.

CORROSIVE FUMES

Charging batteries give off corrosive fumes. These are especially harmful to electronics, so never store or mount electronic equipment inside or even near the battery compartment. This is not so much a safety concern as an economic one.

FUSE

Normally adequate wiring can become a fire hazard if it becomes overloaded. Dampness and motion make boat wiring especially susceptible to unexpected "shorts" that result in just such an overload. A fuse or breaker acts to prevent this by disconnecting the wire if the current passing through it exceeds a safe level.

Every circuit aboard your boat must have a fuse or breaker in the "hot" wire leg. (The *only* exception *might* be the circuit supplying power to the engine starter motor.) The fuse protects the wire, not the appliances the wire supplies. Fuses and breakers should always be as close to the battery as practical.

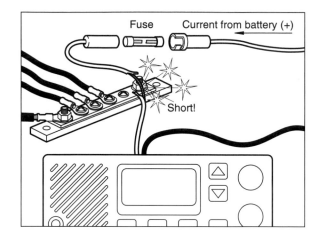

CHAPTER 2

UNDERSTANDING THE BASICS

How many sailors does it take to screw in a light bulb? If you don't want to be the butt of this disparagement, you have to abandon the attitude that everything about electricity is just *too* complicated. *Baseball is complicated.* Compared to the infield fly, the balk, or the ground-rule double, the rules that govern electricity are (invoking a bit of irony here) child's play.

Electricity and baseball have at least one thing in common: nothing worthwhile happens until a runner completes the circuit around the bases. Whether a baseball player is at bat or has managed to advance all the way to third, he is only a *potential* run. We use potential to mean the same thing in electricity. The runner has to return to home plate to score. Electrons are the runners in the electricity game, and until they make the complete circuit, no numbers go up on the scoreboard.

Baseball has its own vocabulary—foul, fly, bunt, double play, pinch hit— but few of us have any difficulty grasping these terms, not even strike, which normally means "to hit sharply," but inexplicably means just the opposite in baseball. A few specialized terms are likewise required to follow the action in the electricity field, but too few to get excited about. Adding a half-dozen new words to your vocabulary will likely be sufficient.

This chapter is essentially the "official rules." In addition to defining terms, it shows how to play the game—including league differences (the electrical equivalent of the designated hitter)—and how to keep score. Nobody likes to read rules, but with electricity you don't get away with a breach just because the umpire misses it. When you break a rule, whether out of ignorance or indifference, there are *always* consequences. Conversely, if you know the rules and follow them, expect a happy outcome.

Most of the terms you need to work on your boat's wiring will come in context, but before we begin building that understanding, we need to lay the four cornerstones. These are the basic concepts of electricity, all named for 18th century scientists.

AMP

Amp, short for ampere, is a measurement of electrical *current*. Just as the Department of Transportation measures traffic flow by counting how many vehicles per hour cross a sensor laid across the highway, we measure the flow of electricity in a wire by counting the number of electrons per second that pass a sensor.

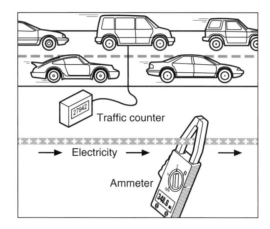

VOLT

Volt is a measurement of *potential*. Potential is not how many cars are on the road, but how many people own cars. The more drivers in downtown office buildings at 4:59, the greater the potential for the traffic flow to be heavier (or last longer) when we flip the switch at 5:00. Likewise, higher voltage forces a greater flow of electrons.

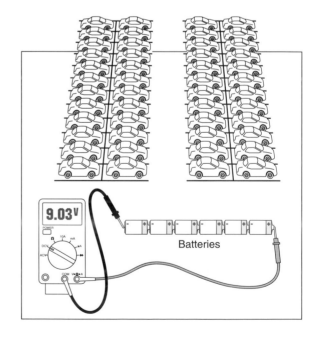

OHM

Ohm is a measurement of *resistance*. A six-lane highway is a good *conductor* of rush-hour traffic, but funnel that down to one lane and traffic nearly stops. Or change the road from straight, smooth asphalt to winding, rutted dirt and the rate of travel drops to a crawl. The flow of electrons is similarly conducted or resisted based on the size and composition of conductors.

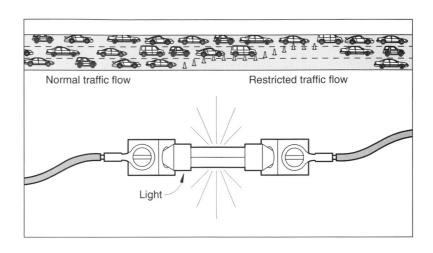

Normal traffic flow   Restricted traffic flow

Light

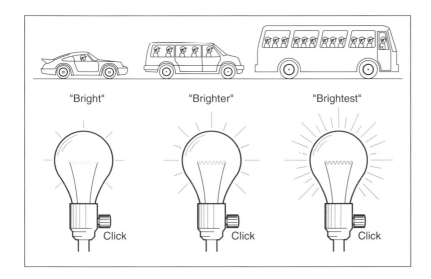

"Bright"   "Brighter"   "Brightest"

Click   Click   Click

WATT

Watt is a measurement of *power*. It is the rate at which work gets done. For example, consider how many people the road system transports from their offices to their homes between 5:00 and 6:00 P.M. Assuming the roads have sufficient capacity, we can increase that rate of "work" by putting more cars on the road or by putting more people in each car. Increasing either volts (force) or amps (current) increases electrical power.

THREE-PART HARMONY

Buy a roll of one hundred 33-cent postage stamps and the cost will be $33. Expressing this everyday calculation as the equation E = N x P (expenditure = number x price) doesn't make it any more complicated. Change the letters and this very same equation expresses how the electrical measurements defined above are related. If you can compute the cost of a book of stamps, you have all the math skill necessary to do electrical calculations.

OHM'S LAW

Understanding the relationship between current, voltage (potential), and resistance is essential to almost every electrical problem or project you might take on. Fortunately, this relationship is dead simple: an increase in voltage increases current; an increase in resistance decreases current. To be specific, *current is directly proportional to voltage and inversely proportional to resistance.* This is Ohm's Law.

If this sounds confusing to you, it isn't. An identical law governs your personal economics—namely, the amount of anything you can buy is directly proportional to how much money you have available and inversely proportional to price. Our postage-stamp equation shows this relationship more clearly rewritten as N = E / P. Doubling the expenditure (E) doubles the number (N) of stamps you buy. Doubling the price (P) cuts N in half.

The equivalent equation for Ohm's Law is I = V / R, where I stands for current, V for voltage, and R for resistance. (We don't use C for current because I is the conventional abbreviation.) To use Ohm's Law, current must always be in amps, abbreviated as A; voltage always in volts, abbreviated as V; and resistance always in ohms, abbreviated as Ω.

If we apply 1 volt to a circuit having 1 ohm of resistance, 1 amp of current will flow (1 V / 1 Ω = 1 A). Increase the voltage to 12 volts, and the current increases proportionally to 12 amps (12 V / 1 Ω = 12 A). Raise the resistance to 6 ohms, and the current flow in the circuit is reduced to 2 amps (12 V / 6 Ω = 2 A).

When we want to calculate resistance rather than current, we rearrange the equation to R = V / I. For voltage calculations, the form becomes V = I x R, or simply V = IR. This latter is the easiest to commit to memory.

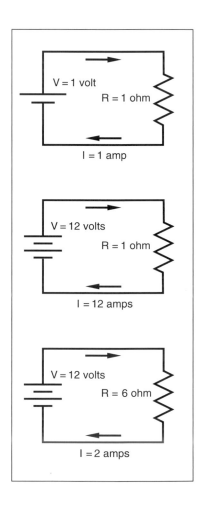

POWER

Power is the rate of doing work. The more powerful an engine is, for example, the more work it can do (i.e., push a larger boat or push a boat faster). The unit of measurement for mechanical power is usually *horsepower*, but for electricity we use the *watt*. The higher the wattage of a light bulb, the more light we expect from it.

Electrical power is derived by multiplying voltage times current. The shorthand for this relationship is P = V x I, where P stands for power, V for voltage, and I for current. If we want the power in watts—and we always do—then the voltage has to be in volts and the current in amps.

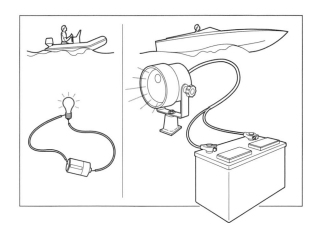

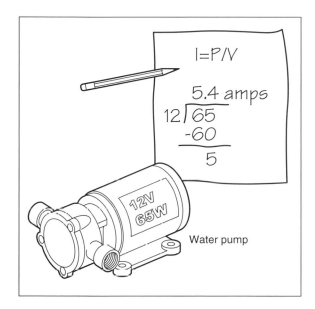

Water pump

As with Ohm's Law, we can write the power equation three ways, depending on what we want to calculate:

$$P = V\,I$$
$$V = P\,/\,I$$
$$I = P\,/\,V$$

The first form is the easiest to remember, but the last is the one you will use most often. Light bulbs and most other electrical equipment are rated in watts, but as you will soon see, we are more often concerned with how much current an appliance draws. To determine that, we simply divide the specified wattage by the electrical system voltage. A 25-watt cabin lamp in a 12-volt system will draw a little more than 2 amps when it is on (25 W / 12 V = 2.08 A).

LOAD CALCULATIONS

Now is a good time to calculate the current draw of every electrical item aboard. You will need this to determine appropriate battery capacity, alternator size, or solar panel benefit. Sometimes current requirements are specified, but more often the rating is in watts. List every appliance aboard, then divide its rated wattage by 12 to get its average current draw.

Note that some high-draw components are rated in kilowatts (kW). A kilowatt is 1,000 watts. So a starter motor shown in your engine manual as 1.8 kW has a current draw of 150 amps (1,800 W / 12 V). Electric windlasses have similar current demands.

Enter the loads into a chart similar to the one shown. We will return to this chart in Chapter 3. The loads depicted in the illustration are typical and may be used to approximate the load of any appliance for which you are unable to locate actual specifications.

TYPICAL 12-VOLT POWER CONSUMPTION

Device	Amps	Device	Amps
Anchor light	0.8	Radar	4.0
Anchor windlass	150.0	Reading light	
Autopilot (above deck)	0.7	—halogen (10w)	0.8
Bilge blower	6.5	Refrigerator	5.0
Cabin fan (efficient)	0.2	Running lights	2.5
Cabin fan (oscillating)	1.2	Running lights	
Cabin light		—Tricolor	0.8
—fluorescent (8w)	0.7	Spotlight	10.0
Cabin light		Tape deck	1.0
—incandescent (25w)	2.1	Television (13-inch)	3.5
Chart light (10w)	0.8	Toilet	40.0
Compass light	0.1	Speed log	0.1
Deck lights	6.0	SSB (receive)	2.5
Depth sounder	0.2	SSB (transmit)	30.0
Gas detector	0.3	Starter	
GPS	0.5	—diesel (1,800w)	150.0
Ham radio (receive)	2.5	VCR	1.0
Ham radio (transmit)	30.0	VCR	2.0
Inverter—standby	0.2	VHF (receive)	0.5
Microwave (600w)	100.0	VHF (transmit)	5.0
Pump—bilge	15.0	Waste treatment	45.0
Pump—freshwater	6.0	Weatherfax	1.0
Pump—shower sump	2.0	Wind indicator	0.1
Pump—washdown	6.0		

DESERT ALGEBRA

If your knowledge of algebra has been buried by the sands of time, you can rely on these two pyramids to keep the equations straight. Putting your finger over the variable you are trying find will reveal the arithmetic required. For example, cover I in the Ohm's Law pyramid and what remains is V over R: I = V / R. Cover P in the power pyramid and you are left with V I: P = V x I. If these work for you, don't be reluctant to rely on them.

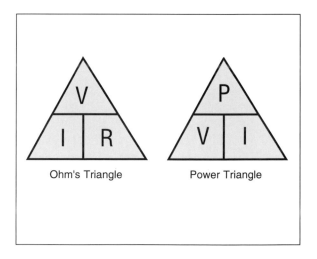

Ohm's Triangle   Power Triangle

It is no coincidence that batteries have two terminals and appliances have two leads. Connecting one lead to the battery's positive terminal and one to the negative provides the closed loop necessary for electrons to flow. This loop is called a circuit.

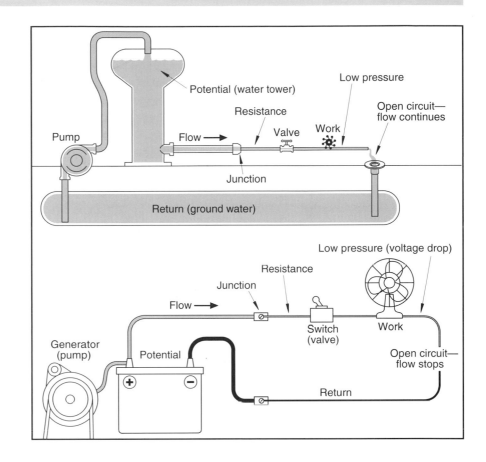

NOT LIKE WATER

Plumbing offers some useful insights into the invisible flow of electricity. You can see what makes a water wheel spin. The impact of wire size is clearer when likened to pipes. The concept of voltage can be easier to grasp when thought of as the electrical equivalent of water pressure. In fact, as long as we keep the plumbing system closed, water works pretty well as an analogy. But as soon as we open the circuit, we discover a major difference between the flow of water and the flow of electricity. As every homeowner knows, water flows out of an open pipe until we shut off or exhaust the supply. In contrast, when we open an electrical circuit, the flow of electricity stops. Not a single electron drips out of the end of the wire.

BOYS WILL BE BOYS

Teenagers offer a better analogy. A high-school gymnasium full of teenage boys at one end, girls at the other, separated by a partition, is essentially a battery. Because the boys are naturally attracted to the girls, we have potential—voltage—but nothing will happen unless the boys can find a path to the girls' side of the "battery." Give the gym an outside corridor connecting both ends—a circuit—and the boys will race from their end of the gym to the girls' end. Unless a chaperon breaks the circuit by closing the corridor door, this "current" continues until the battery is dead, i.e., until the boys' side is empty and the girls' side is full of couples.

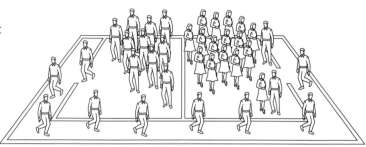

POLARITY

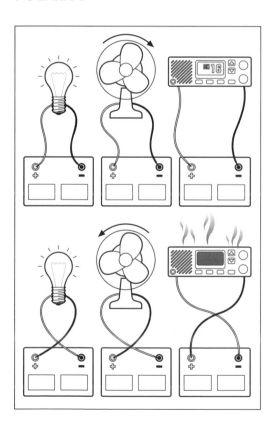

By convention we think of an electrical current as flowing from positive to negative, but the flow of electrons is actually from the negative or ground terminal to the battery's positive terminal. Either way, reversing connections to a circuit reverses the direction of the current flow. While lighting and heating appliances generally operate the same when polarity is reversed, most 12-volt motors run backwards, and electronics will, at best, simply fail to operate and may be damaged or destroyed. For 12-volt components to operate as designed, the lead marked with a "+" must always be connected to the positive side of the circuit.

OPEN AND CLOSED

An electrical circuit provides a continuous path from the positive terminal of a power source to its negative terminal. By this narrow definition, when we break that path we no longer have a circuit. Fortunately, circuit has come to mean any configuration of electrically connected components. A circuit that allows the flow of current is designated as a *closed circuit*. When a break in the circuit interrupts the flow of current, the circuit is *open*.

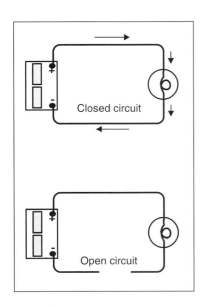

SERIES

When the entire current flow must pass through every component in a circuit, the components are all connected *in series*. Components in a series circuit are connected end-to-end like railroad cars.

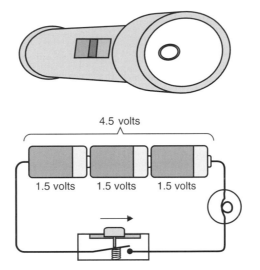

For power sources connected in series—dry cells dropped into the barrel of a flashlight, for example—the total voltage is the sum of the individual voltages. Each dry cell has a voltage of 1.5 volts, so a three-cell flashlight is operating at 4.5 volts.

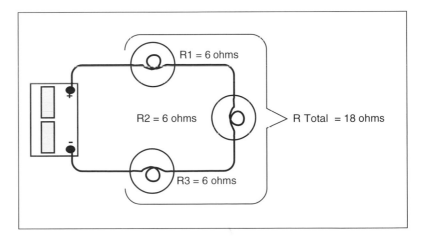

Similarly, the total resistance of loads connected in series is the sum of the individual loads. We calculated earlier that a 12-volt, 25-watt incandescent bulb draws about 2 amps, so by Ohm's Law the bulb's resistance is 6 ohms (12 V / 2 A). If we connect three bulbs in series, the total resistance is 18 ohms.

PARALLEL

When a component is connected in such a way that there is an alternative path for the current to follow, that component is connected *in parallel*. Parallel connections, in their simplest configuration, look like ladder rungs.

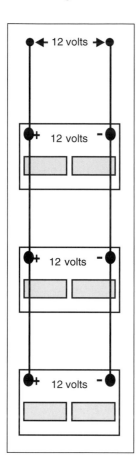

Source voltages don't aggregate in parallel. Connecting batteries in parallel—which you do every time you switch your battery-selector switch to BOTH—simply creates a "bigger" 12-volt battery, one with a capacity (detailed in the next chapter) equal to the sum of the individual battery ratings.

The total resistance of loads connected in parallel is a combination of their individual resistances, but not a direct sum. Rather, the reciprocal of the total resistance is equal to the sum of the reciprocals of the resistance in each branch. This sounds infinitely more complicated than it is. For once, the equation is clearer:

$$\frac{1}{R_T} = \frac{1}{R_1} + \frac{1}{R_2} + \frac{1}{R_3}$$

The reciprocal of total resistance of our three light bulbs connected in parallel is $1/6 + 1/6 + 1/6$, or $1/2$, so the total resistance is 2 ohms. *The resistance of loads in parallel is always less than the resistance of the smallest load.*

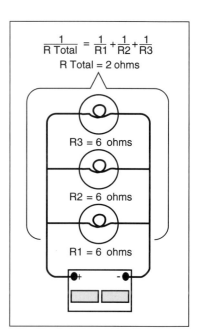

EXTRA CREDIT

WE HAVE ALREADY CALCULATED that a 25-watt, 12-volt cabin lamp draws about 2 amps and has a resistance of about 6 ohms. Three such lamps wired in series would have a combined resistance of 18 ohms. From Ohm's Law, a circuit with 18 ohms resistance connected to a 12-volt battery will draw 0.67 amps (12 V / 18 Ω). Since the definition of a series circuit is that the entire current passes through every component, only 0.67 amps passes through the bulbs—probably insufficient to make them light. It is generally a bad idea to put more than one load in series. We do put switches and fuses in series with the load because we want them to open the circuit.

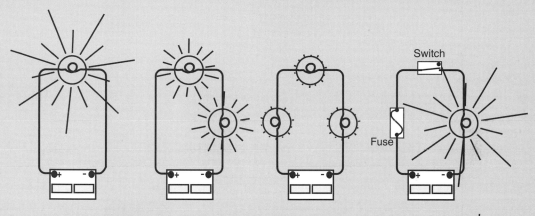

Multiple loads on a circuit are almost always connected in parallel. Connected this way, our three lights will each burn brightly. Since each is drawing 2 amps, the total current must be 6 amps. We calculated the total resistance of three 6-ohm bulbs in parallel as 2 ohms. Ohm's Law— I = V / R—confirms that a 12-volt circuit with 2 ohms total resistance does indeed have a 6-amp current flow (12 V / 2 Ω). The more parallel loads we put on the same circuit, the more current the wires, switches, and fuses must carry. Note that switch A turns off all the lights; switch B affects only one light. Also note that even though each lamp is rated at only 2 amps, we can't use a 2 amp breaker to protect the circuit.

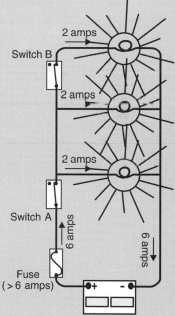

This book is mostly about 12-volt DC, but most modern boats also have AC (alternating current) circuits, whether powered by a cord from a dock outlet, an inverter wired to the ship's battery, or an onboard AC generator. Alternators also generate alternating current. Most of the rules that govern direct current, including Ohm's Law, are equally applicable to alternating current, but the AC league plays the game a little differently.

MAGNETISM AND CURRENT

Electric current and magnetism are related. Much like moving steel shavings on top of a piece of paper by passing a magnet underneath, electrons inside a wire can be induced to move by passing a magnet near the wire. This is exactly how all generators "create" electricity. Coils of wire surround a magnet, and when the magnet spins, it induces a current flow in the wire.

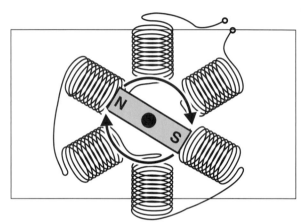

CURRENT

A charged battery has excess electrons in one side and a shortage of electrons in the other. Connect the two sides and electrons flow through the circuit in one direction—like water through a hose. Direct current is, by definition, a one-way flow of electrons.

In an AC circuit electrons don't flow; they do the two-step. Close an AC circuit, and for an instant the electrons start through the circuit just like DC. But back at the generator the positive pole of the spinning magnet is followed by the negative pole, which induces the electrons to flow in the opposite direction. This has the same effect as reversing the battery connections in a DC circuit. And just as the current starts to flow in the new direction, along comes the positive pole in the generator and reverses the direction again.

Alternating current, by definition, reverses direction at regular intervals. Electricity generated by U.S. power companies reverses direction 120 times *per second*.

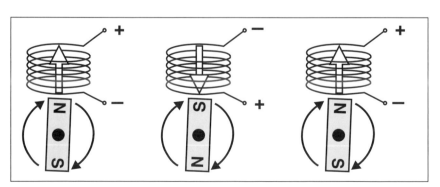

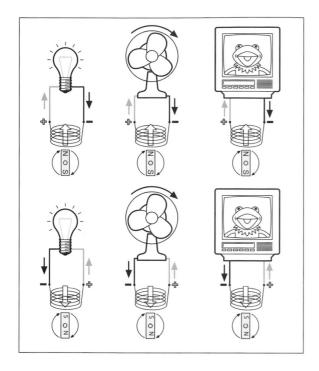

POLARITY

Since current is flowing one direction then the other through AC circuits, the function of AC components, in contrast to their DC counterparts, is unaffected by reversing connections. But while AC components are oblivious to polarity, this emphatically does not mean you can be, too. To the contrary, reversed AC polarity is extremely dangerous, particularly aboard a boat, and must always be avoided (see Chapter 8).

LOADS

How, you might wonder, does alternating current do any work if the electrons are more or less jogging in place? Consider a light bulb illuminated by connecting it to a battery: if you reverse the connections, the bulb still lights. In an AC circuit this reversal happens too fast for the eye to see anything more than perhaps a flicker as the light goes off and back on 120 times per second. In fact, if the bulb is incandescent, the white-hot filament doesn't have time to cool during the "off" times, so the bulb glows steadily even though current is only flowing through the filament intermittently—not unlike propelling a play yard swing with intermittent shoves. And as with the swing, the shove can be in either direction.

VOLTAGE

Ohm's Law tells us that in a circuit with a resistance of 1 ohm, voltage in volts will be equal to current in amps ($V = I \times 1$ or $V = I$). So if the current is alternating, the voltage must be also. Yet an AC voltmeter will register a steady voltage of somewhere between 115 and 125 volts when its probes are inserted into a 120-volt outlet. What's going on?

Since both positive and negative voltages (relative to ground) induce a current to flow, and AC circuits don't care which way the current flows, the AC voltmeter ignores polarity and registers all voltage as positive, which henceforth we shall do also. The meter also averages the voltage which, to yield a mean reading of 120 volts, is oscillating between 0 and a peak of about 170 volts. Fortunately we don't need to be concerned with these oscillations; average voltage (and current) satisfies our needs.

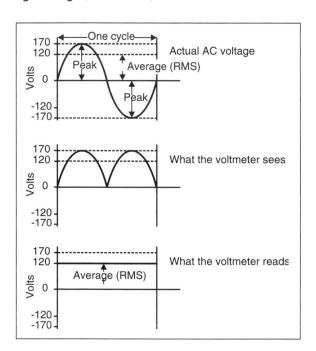

POWER FACTOR

The oscillating voltage of AC power does require one consolation. Some components in a circuit, most notably coils, oppose any *change* in current. This isn't resistance as defined earlier—it is called *reactance*—but it alters the relationship between voltage and current in AC circuits. Voltage times current gives us power in watts ($P = V \times I$) for a DC circuit, but an AC component of a specified wattage may draw more current to compensate for the added load imposed by reactance. For AC, the power in watts is equal to volts times amps times a power factor (PF). In equation form this is $P = V \times I \times PF$, or more often $I = P / (V \times PF)$. PF is 1 when all loads are resistive—which is why we ignore it in DC circuits—but less than 1 when the circuit includes reactive loads. We won't do power factor calculations in this book, but you need to know that applying the DC power equation (PF = 1) to the rated wattage of AC appliances can substantially understate actual power consumption.

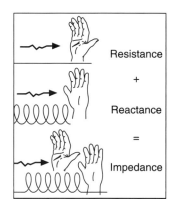

Resistance

+

Reactance

=

Impedance

SAFETY REVISITED

Hand-to-hand resistance through the human body is usually at least 1,000 ohms (check yours by holding the two probes of an ohm meter with wet fingers). Applying Ohm's Law—$I = V / R$—we can see that should you touch both terminals of a 12-volt battery, body resistance limits current flow to 12 milliamps (0.012 amp)—insufficient to pose a serious risk. If, however, you get across an AC circuit, 120 volts will push 0.12 amp through your body. Combined with the pulsating nature of AC current, this is more than twice the level needed to interfere dangerously—even fatally—with heart rhythm. *Work on AC circuits requires extreme caution.*

CHAPTER 3

BATTERY

A storage battery is like a fuel tank. As long as you keep it topped up, the electrical system should keep humming, but let it run out of juice and the system dies.

We don't much care what is going on inside a battery, only that it keeps our electrics running. Unfortunately, where batteries are concerned, ignorance is almost never bliss. About 99.99% of all 12-volt batteries are intended for automobiles, where they are required to give a half-second burst of power several times a day—after which they are immediately and fully replenished by the alternator. A sailboat battery doesn't get such prima donna treatment. We want it to supply all our electrical needs for 24 to 48 hours, then we want to fully replace that 2-day drain with a few minutes of charging time. Such treatment literally murders an automotive battery.

No battery lasts as long or recharges as quickly as we would like, but those designed specifically for periodic as opposed to continuous recharging come the closest. What identifies such batteries? "Marine" on the label is no assurance; many so-called marine batteries are simply relabeled automotive batteries, maybe with the addition of wing-nut terminals and a lifting handle. This might be unscrupulous except that the requirements for a powerboat's starting battery aren't that different from a car battery.

Gel batteries have been increasingly touted as the ideal marine battery, but claims about these should be viewed with some skepticism. Gel cells do have some desirable characteristics, but they are *not* next-generation technology.

The best way to pick a battery to suit your needs is to compare. This chapter explains physical and performance differences among various battery types, and shows how to interpret various battery ratings. It also provides standards for installation and maintenance.

Taking the time to select the right battery, install it well, and maintain it properly is simply good seamanship.

THE BASIC CELL

Batteries are made up of cells connected in series to achieve the desired voltage. For example, a 12-volt automotive or marine battery has 6 cells, each with a fully charged potential of a bit more than 2 volts. Cells convert chemical energy to electrical energy and, in the case of *storage cells*, vice versa.

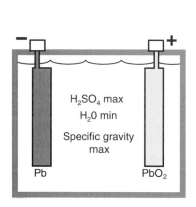

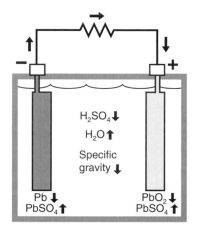

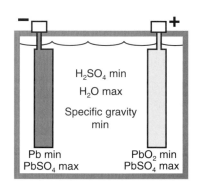

FULLY CHARGED

A cell consists of two dissimilar electrodes immersed in a conductive medium. In a *lead-acid* cell—the kind of cell in automotive and marine batteries—the negative electrode is lead (Pb), the positive electrode is lead dioxide (PbO_2), and the *electrolyte* is sulfuric acid and water ($H_2SO_4 + H_2O$).

DISCHARGING

Free electrons flowing from the lead to the lead dioxide through an external circuit unbalance the chemistry inside the battery, causing the acid to separate into hydrogen (H) and sulfate (SO_4) ions. An ion is a molecule with either extra or missing electrons—the link between chemical energy and electrical energy. Some of the sulfate ions combine with the lead electrode to form lead sulfate ($PbSO_4$). Other sulfate ions displace oxygen from the lead-dioxide electrode and combine with the free lead, also as lead sulfate. The displaced oxygen pairs up with the hydrogen ions to form water (H_2O).

FULLY DISCHARGED

As both electrodes are converted to lead sulfate, they are no longer dissimilar, and the potential between them declines to zero. Or the cell may run out of sulfate ions, leaving the electrodes immersed in pure water, which is not an electrolyte.

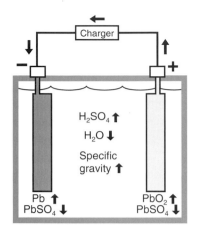

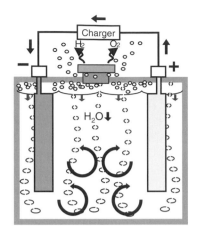

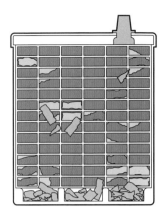

CHARGING

Placing a voltage across the electrodes of the discharged cell reverses the chemical reaction. The water separates into oxygen and hydrogen ions. The sulfate ions separate from the lead and recombine with the hydrogen into sulfuric acid. At the positive electrode, free oxygen recombines with the lead.

GASSING

When the charging current is too strong, some of the hydrogen and oxygen molecules from the decomposing water are released as gases, causing the charging cell to percolate. The rising bubbles have the desirable effect of improving the cell's acceptance of charging current by mixing the electrolyte—which tends to stratify—but as they escape into the air, they lower the water level in the cell. It is essential to closely monitor the fluid level in wet cells, especially when they are deeply discharged and/or rapidly charging.

SHEDDING

Because lead, lead dioxide, and lead sulfate have different densities, the transformation from one to the other and back again causes the plates to expand and contract. In much the same way that heat and cold erode the face of a stone cliff, the surfaces of the plates shed some active material with each discharge cycle. The battery loses the use of this disconnected material, resulting in slightly reduced capacity with each discharge cycle.

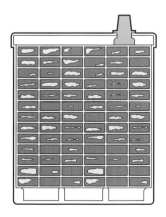

PLATE SULFATION

Sulfates that form on the plates during discharge are initially soft and readily separated from the lead with a charging current. In the absence of a charging current, sulfates begin to crystallize (harden) in a matter of hours. Sulfate crystals are not easily reconverted, and the battery suffers a permanent loss of capacity. Sulfation occurs when a battery is left in a discharged state—even partially discharged. It is analogous to rust forming on idle machinery. Even a small charging current inhibits plate sulfation.

INEFFICIENCIES

Drain 10 gallons from a full, 10-gallon fuel tank and it takes exactly 10 gallons to refill it. "Refilling" a storage cell is not so straightforward. The chemical reaction during discharge is the natural one, like water flowing down-hill. Charging is an "uphill" flow, and energy is lost to overcoming opposition. On average, expect to put back about 20 percent more energy than you take out.

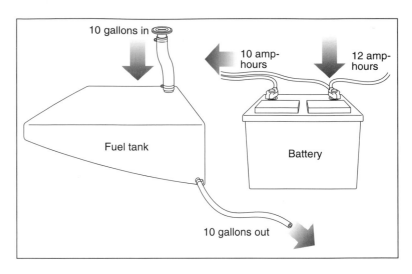

10 gallons in

10 amp-hours

12 amp-hours

Fuel tank

Battery

10 gallons out

BATTERIES

Batteries are technically a series of cells, although we ignore that distinction when we refer to a single dry cell as a flashlight battery.

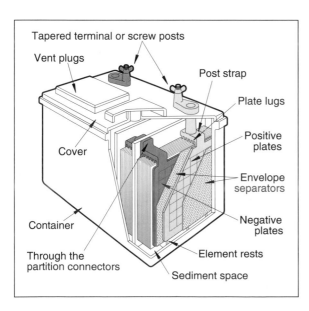

Tapered terminal or screw posts

Vent plugs

Post strap

Plate lugs

Positive plates

Cover

Envelope separators

Container

Negative plates

Element rests

Through the partition connectors

Sediment space

INTERNAL CONSTRUCTION

Voltage depends on the nature of the chemical reaction, so all lead-acid cells have fully charged potential of about 2.1 volts. Amperage, on the other hand, depends on how much chemical reaction is going on, which is mostly dependent upon the amount of electrode material. In lead-acid batteries, the electrodes are constructed as rectangular plates, each reinforced with a conductive grid. Lead and lead-dioxide plates are interleaved, like shuffled cards, and electrically insulated from each other with porous separators. All the positive (lead-dioxide) plates are connected electrically, as are all the negative (lead) plates. Individual cells—six of them in a 12-volt battery—are electrically connected in series, either internally or on top of the battery.

PLATE THICKNESS

All lead-acid batteries shed plate material with each discharge cycle. Naturally, thicker plates last longer. When thick, dense plates shed, it exposes inner plate surfaces the electrolyte previously did not reach, so that early in the battery's life the capacity does not decline and may even increase. For deep-cycling, you want thick plates.

But thick plates also react more slowly with the electrolyte, making thin plates better at delivering a lot of current at once. Likewise, thin plates accept a faster charge.

SPONGY LEAD

The lead used in lead-acid batteries is less like a slab and more like a sponge. Porosity facilitates chemical reaction by giving the lead more surface contact with the electrolyte. Low-density lead helps a battery deliver large currents, but it is also fragile and, by definition, there is less active material. High-density lead is more durable and less susceptible to shedding. The denser the lead, the more discharge cycles a battery will tolerate. A sure sign of lead density is relative battery weight.

SELF DISCHARGE

Wet-cell plate grids are lead but alloyed with a small amount of antimony to strengthen them. The dissimilarity between the lead and antimony sets up small internal currents which allow the battery to self-discharge. In warm weather an idle wet cell will lose as much as 1 percent of its charge per day, and more in the tropics. This means even a fully charged wet cell will be 30-percent discharged if idle for a summer month. A battery in this state—discharged and idle—will lose capacity to sulfation.

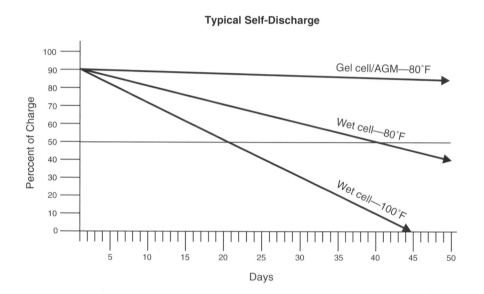

Typical Self-Discharge

Because gel and AGM batteries (see pages 27 and 28) do not contain antimony, their self-discharge rates are much lower—typically around 0.1 percent per day.

STARTING OR HOUSE?

BOAT BATTERIES can be categorized by how they will be used. A starting battery performs similarly to an automotive battery, providing a burst of current immediately countered by an input current sufficient to restore the battery to full charge. Starting batteries are sometimes selected for other high-current requirements such as powering a windlass, but such a choice assumes that the engine will be running when the battery is under load.

A house battery is expected to provide on-demand power to lights, pumps, fans, and electronics, delivering lower current levels but over a much longer time period. House batteries are routinely discharged to about half of capacity before being recharged.

Boats often have both starting and house batteries aboard. A house battery can be used as a starting battery without consequence (provided it is up to the task), but most starting batteries will not fully recover from even a single deep discharge as a house battery.

BATTERY CHOICES

Twelve-volt batteries are not all the same. Which will be your best choice depends entirely on what you expect from it.

AUTOMOTIVE—CONVENTIONAL FLOODED

Standard automotive batteries—what every garage and auto-supply house sells—are conventional flooded batteries. So are marine batteries designated as "starting" batteries. They have thin plates and low-density lead to maximize momentary output, and they are all designed to operate at at least 95 percent of full charge.

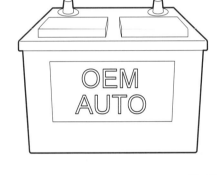

A boat's motion will literally shake the lead out of the internal grids in a cheap automotive battery, but there is no reason that a good-quality battery designed to start your car cannot provide the same function in your boat. However, if you deeply discharge an automotive battery—either accidentally or by design, you shorten its life. A conventional flooded battery may fail completely after as few as 20 discharge cycles, making this type unsuitable as a house battery—even occasionally. And because automotive batteries typically have high self-discharge rates, they are a poor choice even as a starting battery for a boat used infrequently.

MAINTENANCE-FREE

A maintenance-free battery is essentially a conventional flooded battery in a sealed case. As long as the rate of charge is kept low, the generated free oxygen and hydrogen are trapped inside the battery to recombine into water rather than escape as gasses. A safety valve allows excess pressure to escape, and maintenance-free batteries are given extra electrolyte to offset occasional venting. Maintenance-free batteries work well in cars where the charge voltage is relatively low (typically about 13.8 volts), but the voltage of almost all boat charging systems will cause maintenance-free batteries to vent and lose water. Since they have no fill caps—an identifying characteristic—water cannot be added, so these batteries are likely to have a short life. It is rarely feasible to lower charge voltage to accommodate a maintenance-free starting battery, since this would result in chronic undercharging of the house batteries. Maintenance-free batteries are simply unsuitable for a boat.

No fill caps

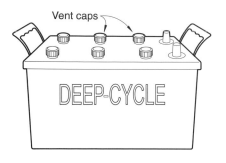

Vent caps

DEEP-CYCLE

No spill—can be used on its side

GEL

No fill caps

GEL CELL

The electrolyte in gel cells has the consistency of butter. Coated plates and separators are compressed tightly together like a multilayered sandwich. Because the electrolyte is a semisolid, it is unable to diffuse through thick, dense plates, so gel cell plates are thin and less dense. Tight lamination of plates and separators makes the assembly sufficiently rigid that grids can be pure lead or lead-calcium, eliminating antimony and thereby reducing self-discharge to less than 0.1 percent. Such a minuscule self-discharge rate means gel cells can be left idle for weeks or even months with no adverse effect.

Like a conventional flooded battery, gel cells can deliver a lot of current quickly, so they are suitable for starting or for powering high-current appliances (windlass, inverter, etc.). As a house battery, a gel cell has about $1/4$ the life *expectancy* of a similar quality deep-cycle battery, but a good-quality gel cell will deliver its 500 or so half cycles (to the 50% discharge level) without any care. Because a gel cell accepts a charge more quickly than a deep-cycle battery, it will be at a higher charge state for a given amount of charging time. Unless the deep-cycle battery gets additional charging time, the resulting sulfation can reduce its *actual* life to fewer cycles than the gel cell delivers.

Other advantages of the gel cell for a sailboat are that the battery is sealed so it cannot spill acid even if inverted, and it can survive submersion. The most significant fault is intolerance of overcharging. Charging voltage above 14.1 volts will cause a gel cell to gas, which it must not do. A not-uncommon regulator failure can quickly destroy gel cells, much like a failed shroud results in a broken mast.

DEEP CYCLE

True deep-cycle batteries have thick, high-density plates. Pound-for-pound they won't deliver as much instantaneous current as a conventional battery, but they are tolerant of repeated deep discharge. Top quality deep-cycle batteries are capable of being discharged to half their rated capacity more than a thousand times.

Most deep-cycle batteries are intended for golf carts and fork lifts. On a boat they are the top choice for house batteries *provided they are properly charged and maintained*. Because the plates are thick and dense, it takes a while for the electrolyte to diffuse into the interior of the plates, so deep-cycle batteries are painfully slow to reach full charge. But full charge is essential to prevent sulfation and allow the battery to achieve its potential.

Deep-cycle batteries typically gas vigorously during charging, which helps diffuse the electrolyte but also means the lost water must be replaced. Gassing can also be corrosive to nearby metals.

SCALES DON'T LIE

Ignore "deep-cycle" labels. Check the weight. There is a direct relationship between relative battery weight and potential battery life; the heavier a battery is (relative to others with the same case dimensions), the more discharge cycles you can expect it to deliver.

ABSORBED GLASS MAT

The absorbed-glass-mat battery (AGM) is a variation of gel-cell technology. The plates sandwich glass-mat separators that have been saturated with electrolyte. As with the gel cell, this type of battery requires thin plates compressed tightly against the wet mat. AGM batteries are extremely efficient and have low self-discharge rates, but they operate even closer to the edge than gel batteries. Overcharging will dry out the mat separators and destroy an AGM battery in short order.

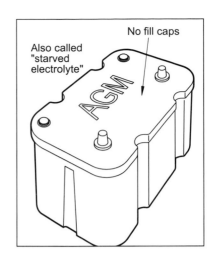

SELECTION CHART

Any 12-volt battery can power your electrical system—for a time. The generalizations in this chart should help you select the best type for your specific requirements.

BATTERY SELECTION CHART						
Type	**Automotive**	**Maintenance-Free**	**Deep-Cycle Marine**	**Golf Cart**	**Gel**	**AGM**
Initial Cost	Low	Low	High	Low	High	High
Amp-Hours	85 (Group 27)	85 (Group 27)	105 (Group 27) 225 (8D)	220 (T-105)	85 (Group 27)	95 (Group 27)
Deep Cycles	20	20	400 to 2,000	700	400 to 1,000	400 to 1,000
Cranking Capacity	Good	Good	Fair	Fair	Good	Good
Durability	Variable	Variable	Very good	Very good	Excellent	Excellent
Neglect Tolerance	Poor	Fair	Poor	Poor	Good	Good
Overcharge Tolerance	Good	Poor	Good	Good	Poor	Poor
Long-Term Cost	High	High	Low	Lowest	Low	Low
Best Use	Starting	None	House- Crusing boat	House- Cruising boat	Starting Inverter Windlass House- Weekend boat	Starting Inverter Windlass House- Weekend boat

CAPACITY

A fter you decide on the type of battery, you need to determine what size you need. Unfortunately, battery ratings seem designed to mislead.

AMP-HOURS

For house batteries, the only useful rating is amp-hours (Ah), which is a measurement of current flow over time. One amp flowing for one hour is 1 amp-hour. One amp flowing for two hours is 2 Ah. Two amps flowing for one hour is also 2 Ah. Amps times hours gives you amp-hours.

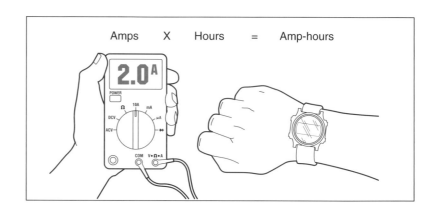

Amps X Hours = Amp-hours

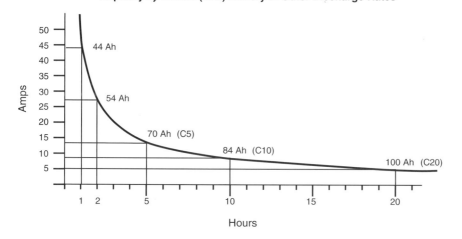

Capacity of 100 Ah (C20) Battery at Other Discharge Rates

A 5-gallon jug holds 5 gallons, but battery capacity isn't as exact. The faster you "pour" energy from a battery, the less of it you can get. For example, a battery capable of delivering 5 amps for 20 hours will deliver 50 amps for no more than an hour. In the first instance its capacity is 100 Ah, in the second, only 50. Conversely, slow the discharge rate to 2 amps and you might get 120 amp-hours or more from this battery.

Batteries in the U.S. are almost always rated for a 20-hour discharge—specifically, the current the battery should be capable of supplying over a 20-hour period before the cell voltage falls from 2.1 volts (fully charged) to 1.75 volts (dead). This is called a C20 rate. Batteries manufactured in other countries are often rated for a 10-hour discharge (C10 rate) and some deep-cycle batteries are rated for 5 hours (C5). The good news is that if you purchase a battery thinking the rate is C20 but it is actually one of the other ratings, the battery will have more capacity than you expected, not less.

Actual capacity also depends on temperature. U.S. ratings normally specify 80°F (27°C). As the temperature of a battery declines, so does its capacity. At freezing, battery capacity is reduced by about a third; i.e., a 100-Ah-rated battery will deliver only about 65 Ah of current at 32°F (0°C).

CYCLE LIFE

After amp-hours, the most valuable specification for a house battery is cycle life. It is also the most misleading. A battery completes one cycle when it is completely discharged then fully recharged. With each cycle, a battery loses some capacity. Manufacturers determine a battery's tolerance of deep discharge by counting the cycles until the capacity of the tested battery has declined to half its rating. A cell voltage of 1.75 volts is the standard for fully discharged, and this is the discharge depth manufacturers should use. Some do, but others discharge their batteries to only 50 percent. This has the (not unexpected) effect of approximately doubling the rated cycle life. When comparing batteries be sure you know the testing methods for both.

Lest you think that rating cycle life using the 50-percent-discharge method is more accurate anyway because that is the usual target discharge level for house batteries, note that the "life" of the test battery extends until capacity has halved. In practice, a battery that falls to even 75 percent of rated capacity will fail to meet power requirements and will need replacement. This optimism is somewhat offset by the life-shortening effect of deeper cycles, so cycle life determined by the full-discharge method is likely to better estimate real-world results. Limiting the depth of discharge dramatically extends the life of a battery.

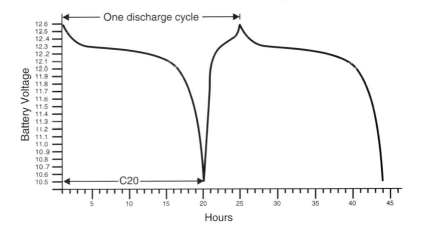

COLD-CRANKING AMPS

Cold-cranking amps (CCA) is the number of amps a battery at 0°F (-18°C) can sustain for 30 seconds without the cell voltage dropping below 1.2 volts. Unfortunately, this rating is also misleading. Even under starter load you don't really want to draw battery voltage down to 7.2 volts (1.2 V per cell). Use cold-cranking amps rating primarily to compare batteries; the higher the CCA, the heavier the starter loads the battery can handle.

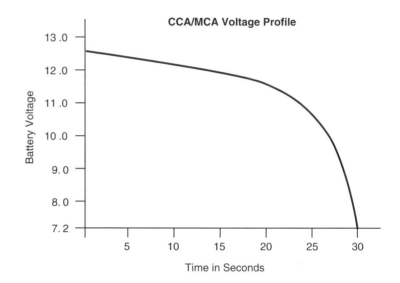

MARINE-CRANKING AMPS

Marine-cranking amps (MCA) is determined in exactly the same way as cold-cranking amps, except that the temperature is 32°F (0°C). Some see MCA as a more meaningful rating because pleasure boats are mostly used in warm conditions. More cynical types see it as a marketing ploy to inflate the CCA by about 25 percent. Either way, it adds confusion to a rating package that is already bewildering. When comparing batteries, be sure you compare MCA numbers only to other MCAs.

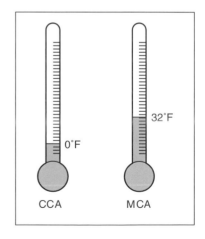

RESERVE MINUTES

Automotive batteries are not expected (by the maker) to supply power for hours, so their labels appropriately show reserve minutes rather than amp-hours. The idea behind reserve minutes—also called reserve capacity—is how long a fully charged battery will keep the engine running and the lights on if the alternator fails, or how long it will power emergency flashers if you break down. The rating is the number of minutes a battery can sustain a constant load—usually 25 amps (called R25)—at 80°F (27°C) before cell voltage falls from 2.1 volts to 1.75 volts. The reserve minutes rating can be helpful for evaluating a battery to be dedicated to a high-load use, such as powering an inverter or a long-range transmitter.

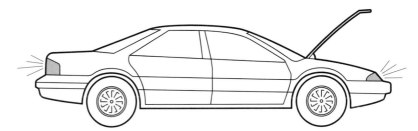

SIZING BATTERIES

How big should your batteries be?

LOAD CALCULATION REDUX

The required capacity for house batteries depends entirely on how much electrical gear you have aboard, how much power each item requires, and how much you use them. In the last chapter you should have listed the current requirements of every item aboard. Now we want to expand that to daily amp-hour requirements by factoring in the time each item is in operation. For example, if you have an incandescent light in the main salon that draws 2.1 amps and it is usually illuminated from 7 to 11 P.M., the average daily consumption is 8.4 amp-hours (2.1 A x 4 hours).

Picking another example, if your freshwater pump delivers 3 gallons per minute, and you never use more than 6 gallons per day, run time is around 2 minutes per day. That makes the daily consumption of a 6-amp pump about 0.2 amp-hours (6 A x 1/30 hour).

Calculate daily amp-hours for all your 12-volt appliances, then add them to estimate your total daily amp-hour requirement.

TYPICAL 12-VOLT POWER CONSUMPTION

Device	Amps	Hours of Use	Daily amp-hours
Anchor light	0.8	12	9.6
Anchor windlass	150.0	0.2	30.0
Autopilot (above deck)	0.7	8	5.6
Bilge blower	6.5	0.2	1.3
Cabin fan (2)	0.2	48	9.6
Cabin light—fluorescent (3)	0.7	12	8.4
Cabin light—incandescent (head)	2.1	1	2.1
Chart light (10 W)	0.8	0.5	0.4
Compass light	0.1	0	0
Deck lights	6.0	0.5	3.0
Depth sounder	0.2	8	1.6
Gas detector	0.3	24	7.2
GPS	0.5	8	4.0
Ham radio (receive)	2.5	1	2.5
Ham radio (transmit)	30.0	0.2	6.0
Inverter—standby	0.2	2	0.4
Microwave (600 W)	100.0	0.1	10.0
Pump—bilge	15.0	0	0
Pump—freshwater	6.0	0.03	0.2
Pump—shower sump	2.0	0.05	0.1
Pump—washdown	6.0	0.2	1.2
Radar	4.0	4	16.0
Reading light—halogen (2)	0.8	4	3.2
Refrigerator	5.0	12	60.0
Running lights	2.5	0	0
Running lights—tricolor	0.8	0	0
Spotlight	10.0	0	0
Tape deck	1.0	2	2.0
Television (13-inch)	3.5	2	7.0
Toilet	40.0	0.3	12.0
Speed log	0.1	8	0.8
SSB (receive)	2.5	1	2.5
SSB (transmit)	30.0	0.2	6.0
Starter—diesel (1,800 W)	150.0	0.02	3.0
Strobe	1.0	0	0
VCR	2.0	2	4.0
VHF (receive)	0.5	4	2.0
VHF (transmit)	5.0	0.2	1.0
Waste treatment	45.0	0.05	2.2
Weatherfax	1.0	0.1	0.1
Wind indicator	0.1	8	0.8

Total Daily Consumption   **225.8**

Note that some loads preclude others; i.e., when the anchor light is in use, the running lights are not

THE ALTERNATIVE TO BIGGER BATTERIES

HALVING CONSUMPTION HAS THE SAME EFFECT AS DOUBLING CAPACITY, and it need not reduce comfort or convenience. Consider refrigeration, often the most voracious electrical item aboard. A change in the thickness of the insulation around the box has a nearly direct reciprocal effect on power consumption; i.e., doubling the thickness of the insulation halves the amp-hours the compressor requires. An additional 3 inches (7.62 cm) of foam insulation might easily reduce daily load by 30 or 40 amp-hours, reducing needed battery capacity by 100 amp hours. And foam is much lighter than lead.

How about your interior lighting? Factory-installed incandescent fixtures provide about 13 lumens (a measurement of light output) per watt. Halogen lights are somewhat more efficient at about 20 lumens per watt. Fluorescent lights raise the bar to 50 lumens per watt. Compact fluorescents (called PL tubes) are even more efficient, providing about 65 lumens per watt. Replace a 45-watt incandescent fixture with an Alpenglow 9-watt compact fluorescent unit and you get the same amount of light while reducing power consumption by a startling 80%.

Fans offer a similar opportunity to economize. A standard 12-volt oscillating fan draws about 1.2 amps, but Hella offers energy-efficient fans that move almost as much air, yet draw only 0.2 amps. This reduces the daily drain on the battery by as much as 24 amp-hours (per fan) in hot weather.

Taking economy to the ultimate, foot pumps completely eliminate the 6-amp draw of the freshwater pump, but a look at your consumption chart will show that this probably saves less than 0.5 amp-hours daily. Foot pumps are a good idea on a boat not because they save power but because they save water, also in short supply.

Before you add battery capacity, evaluate your electrical equipment. Efficient appliances don't just save the cost of bigger batteries, they also save—over and over again—with reduced loads on your charging system.

Lowering Battery Capacity Requirements

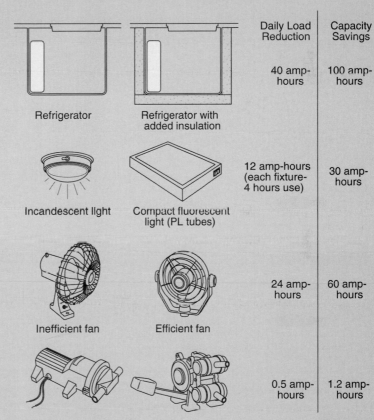

		Daily Load Reduction	Capacity Savings
Refrigerator	Refrigerator with added insulation	40 amp-hours	100 amp-hours
Incandescent light	Compact fluorescent light (PL tubes)	12 amp-hours (each fixture-4 hours use)	30 amp-hours
Inefficient fan	Efficient fan	24 amp-hours	60 amp-hours
		0.5 amp-hours	1.2 amp-hours

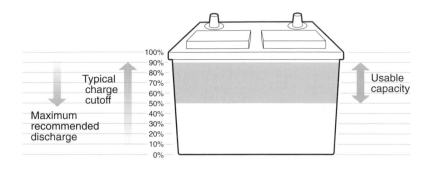

HOUSE BANK

If you limit discharge to about 50% of capacity, you need 2 Ah of capacity for every 1 Ah of consumption between charges. But that assumes you fully recharge the battery after each discharge, which, as you will see in Chapter 7, probably isn't going to happen. A 90% charge level is more likely, so consumption should equate to the battery capacity between a 50% charge level and a 90% level. We can restate this: As a general rule, house battery capacity should be about $2\frac{1}{2}$ times consumption, in amp-hours, between charges. The consumption level in the table requires more than 550 amp-hours of battery capacity.

STARTING BATTERY

The minimum capacity for a starting battery depends on the current requirement of the starter. This is usually specified in the engine manual, but if not, allow about 2 amps per cubic inch of diesel engine displacement; about half that for gasoline engines. An engine in good condition shouldn't crank more than a few seconds, so we are not interested in amp-hours here, just amps. Since charging systems do fail, we want to be able to crank the engine several times without recharging, not just once. A CCA rating of about four times the starter load will give you a dozen normal starts or let you crank a recalcitrant engine for close to two minutes.

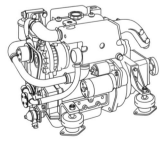 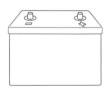

Engine displacement x 2 (cubic inches x 2)   =   Approximate cranking amps
Approximate cranking amps x 4   =   Recommended CCA rating

POWERING INVERTERS

Inverters for powering 120-volt appliances—microwave ovens, VCRs, bread makers, etc.—have become increasingly popular. The current demand of an inverter is similar to that of a starter motor, but you might operate an inverter for minutes or even hours rather than seconds. Solving the power equation for current (I = P / V), we can see that a 1,000-watt inverter (a relatively modest unit) draws 83 amps under full load, and since most inverters are only about 85 percent efficient, the actual draw is closer to 100 amps.

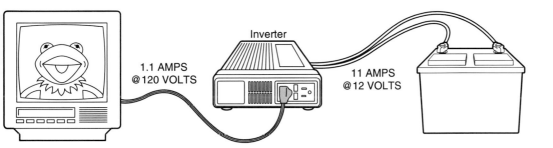

Inverter

1.1 AMPS
@ 120 VOLTS

11 AMPS
@ 12 VOLTS

To determine the actual load your inverter imposes, calculate the amperage at 12 volts for each AC appliance plugged into it. For lighting and heating appliances do this the normal way—by dividing rated watts by 12 (volts). For other appliances the equation needs to include the power factor (see Chapter 2). (If you don't know the actual power factor, use 0.6 for microwave ovens, 0.5 for motorized appliances.) A 600-watt microwave places an 83-amp load on the battery (600 W / [12 V X 0.6]) plus about 15% due to inverter inefficiency.

When the appliance is rated in amps, this is amps at 120 volts, so you must first convert to watts—the amp rating times 120—then reconvert watts to amps at 12 volts by dividing by 12. Those with a bent toward math will see immediately that multiplying AC amps by 10 gives the same result. A TV labeled 1.1 amps will cause your inverter to draw 11 amps from the battery (plus efficiency losses).

Multiply current draw by daily use to get daily consumption. If the microwave above averages 6 minutes of use daily—typical for heating leftovers—it consumes less power than an hour of television. For those 6 minutes, though, it requires a battery capable of continuously supplying close to 100 amps.

Some deep-cycle batteries cannot maintain acceptable voltage at such high discharge levels. A conventional flooded battery can, but it will be damaged by the depth of the discharge if the inverter is in use for very long. Catch 22. This is where gel and AGM batteries excel. But regardless of battery type, using an inverter without the engine running requires lots of battery capacity.

INSTALLATION

Batteries on a sailboat should always be contained in an acid-proof box and secured in such a way that they will stay put even if the boat rolls 360 degrees. Flooded batteries require efficient ventilation to allow the escape of explosive hydrogen gas. Generated oxygen is especially corrosive to nearby electronics.

SERIES

Connecting batteries in series combines their voltages. It is a common practice to use two 6-volt batteries connected in series to provide a 12-volt power source. Besides keeping battery weight manageable, deep-cycle 6-volt batteries are an incredible value (see sidebar).

The rules for series installation are simple: batteries in series must be the same make, model and age to avoid a weaker battery drawing power from a stronger one—to the detriment of both. For the same reason, always replace both batteries at the same time even if only one is bad.

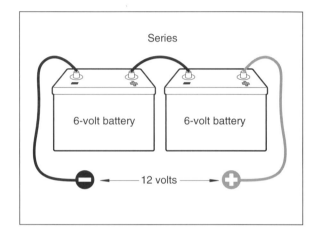

GOLF-CART BATTERIES

GOLF CART BATTERIES are of interest to sailors because they are designed to be discharged all day, then given a charge to prepare them for the next day's gaggle of duffers—a use pattern remarkably similar to what a sailboat's house battery experiences. Good-quality golf-cart batteries last three or four years in this service.

What makes golf cart batteries particularly notable is that they are readily available at very attractive discount prices. The well-respected Trojan T-105, for example, can be purchased for as little as $60. That makes the cost of a 12-volt, 225-amp-hour bank $120. A marine-quality deep-cycle 8D battery of equivalent capacity will run more than twice that amount. An 8D *might* deliver more cycles, but probably not twice as many (the T-105 is independently rated at a more-than-respectable 750 full discharge cycles). This makes a good-quality golf-cart battery the best value in terms of amp-hours for the dollar over the life of the battery, with the not-to-be-dismissed advantage that if some life-ending misfortune befalls your batteries—you forget to keep the water level up, an unnoticed regulator failure boils them dry, a stuck bilge-pump float submerges them—replacement cost is far more palatable.

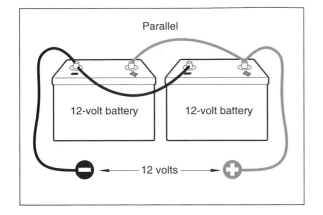

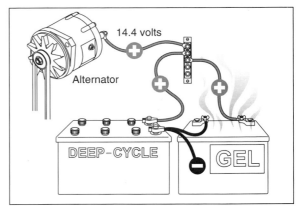

PARALLEL

Connecting batteries in parallel has no effect on voltage, but amperage is combined. Turning the battery-selector switch in your boat to BOTH connects battery (or bank) 1 in parallel with battery (or bank) 2. Many skippers select this setting for engine starting to double the current that would be available to the starter from one battery alone.

Wiring two or more house batteries in parallel to increase amp-hour capacity is also a common practice. Two 100-Ah 12-volt batteries connected in parallel in effect become a 200-Ah 12-volt battery; four provide 400 Ah of capacity.

For starting or other high-amperage use, you can parallel batteries with differing capacities (but not different voltages!) temporarily—through a selector switch—without harm, but the rules for hard-wiring two batteries in parallel are the same as for connecting them in series: batteries in parallel must be the same make, model, and age.

MATCHING

Batteries connected together permanently—in series or parallel—must be identical twins, but what about having a gel battery for starting and a deep-cycle flooded battery for house use? Generally speaking, it is a bad idea. Each requires a different charging regimen. The charge voltage needed to quickly revive a flooded battery—around 14.4 volts—will cook a gel cell, but if you lower charge voltage to 13.8 volts to accommodate the gel cell, the flooded battery will be destroyed by undercharging. Mixing battery types requires the ability to charge them at different levels—a considerable complication and expense. It almost always makes more sense to pick one type—either flooded or gel (or AGM)—and stick with it.

NEGATIVE GROUND

The negative post of all batteries should be connected to "ground" to hold it at 0 potential—relative to earth. This is normally accomplished with a cable between the negative battery post and a bolt on the engine block, which connects the battery to earth through the propeller shaft. We refer to the bolt on the engine as the "grounding lug." Multiple connections to ground should be made to a bus connected to the grounding lug. This is *the main grounding bus.*

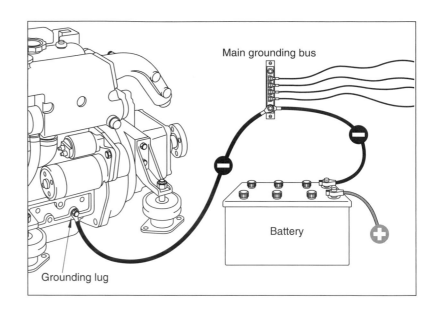

Main grounding bus

Battery

Grounding lug

TEMPERATURE

Charging, especially fast charging, raises the internal temperature of a battery. If the temperature exceeds 120°F (48.4°C), battery life will be shortened. To avoid this, it is essential to mount batteries in a relatively cool location so they can dissipate generated heat. As a general rule, batteries should not be mounted in the engine compartment.

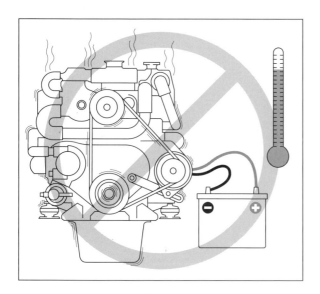

There is no such thing as a no-maintenance battery. All batteries require care if they are to last.

DISCHARGE

The deeper batteries are discharged, the more active material the plates shed, which reduces capacity and shortens the life of the battery. The generally accepted rule of thumb is that the best trade-off between battery capacity and battery life is achieved by limiting discharge to about 50% of capacity. In other words, don't drain more than 50 amp hours from a 100-amp-hour battery before recharging it.

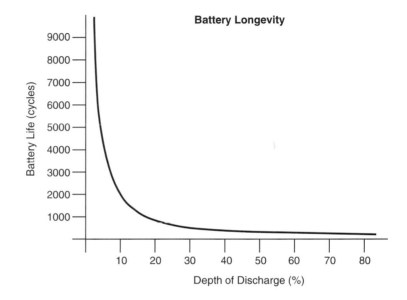

On the other hand, batteries accept higher charging currents at deeper levels of discharge. It takes a lot less charging time to bring a battery from 70% discharged to 50% discharged than from 20% discharged to fully charged, even though the number of amp-hours required is identical. Because the cycle-life curve is relatively flat beyond 50%—meaning that deeper discharges have a decreasing impact on battery life—it can make sense in some circumstances to trade shorter battery life for fewer engine hours or longer intervals between charges.

Under no circumstances should you discharge a battery beyond 80% of capacity or draw the no-load voltage below about 12 volts (2 volts per cell). At discharge levels greater than 80%, cell voltage drops precipitously, and as voltage approaches 0, stronger cells will reverse the polarity of weaker ones, doing irreparable damage to the battery.

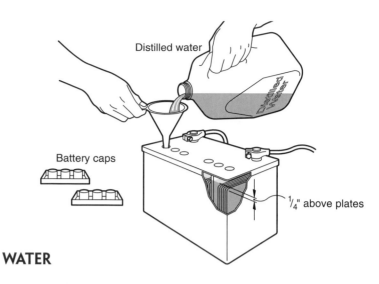

Distilled water

Battery caps

$^1/_4$" above plates

RECHARGING

Leaving a battery in a discharged state—even partially discharged—leads to sulfation and attendant loss of capacity. A good charging regimen will add years of life to a house battery. Battery recharging is covered in detail in Chapter 7.

WATER

Water may be lost to gassing during charging, especially in warm conditions. If the electrolyte level is ever allowed to fall below the top of the plates, all exposed plate area will oxidize and be forever lost to use. Maintain the water level about $^1/_4$ inch above the plates.

To maximize battery life, use only distilled water for topping up; trace minerals and/or chlorine will shorten battery life. Fill cells *after* charging. If you fill them before, expansion during charging can pump electrolyte out on top of the battery, causing a corrosive mess and reducing the acid level inside the battery.

CLEAN AND DRY

Dampness, dirt, or acid on the battery case can create a circuit between the terminals that will drain the battery. Keep the top of the case clean and dry.

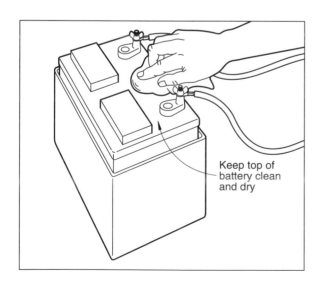

Keep top of battery clean and dry

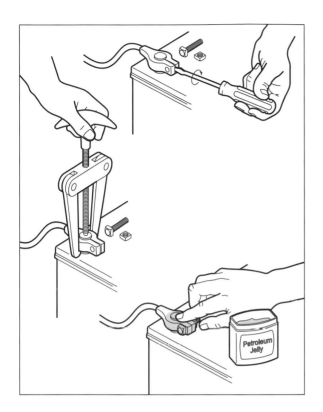

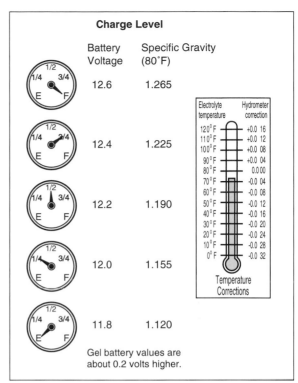

Charge Level

Battery Voltage	Specific Gravity (80°F)
12.6	1.265
12.4	1.225
12.2	1.190
12.0	1.155
11.8	1.120

Gel battery values are about 0.2 volts higher.

Electrolyte temperature	Hydrometer correction
120°F	+0.0 16
110°F	+0.0 12
100°F	+0.0 08
90°F	+0.0 04
80°F	0.0 00
70°F	-0.0 04
60°F	-0.0 08
50°F	-0.0 12
40°F	-0.0 16
30°F	-0.0 20
20°F	-0.0 24
10°F	-0.0 28
0°F	-0.0 32

Temperature Corrections

TERMINAL CORROSION

An inordinate number of electrical system problems stem from corroded battery terminals. If terminals and cable clamps are not bright, remove the clamps by releasing the bolt and spreading the clamp by twisting a screwdriver blade between the jaws. The clamp should slip off. If not, you need a battery-clamp puller. Never pry a cable clamp from a terminal; you risk ruining the battery. The puller is much cheaper.

Always remove the negative cable first and reconnect it last. If the terminals and clamps are heavily corroded, clean them with a wire brush. Polish off light corrosion with a baking-soda paste, then rinse the parts and thoroughly dry them. After they are reassembled, coat both the terminal and the clamp with petroleum jelly (not grease) to prevent future corrosion.

VOLTAGE

With a digital voltmeter you can assess the charge status of a battery by checking the open-circuit voltage. (An analog meter won't do because the difference between fully charged and half charged in a 12-volt battery is less than half a volt.) But don't expect a voltmeter to work like a fuel gauge. Battery voltage continues to rise after charging stops, so an immediate voltage reading will understate the charge status by as much as 0.1 volt—the equivalent of about one eighth of a tank. Similarly, after a heavy discharge battery voltage will "recover" over a period of several hours. Accurate readings are possible only after the battery has rested for 24 hours. In practice, letting the battery stabilize for about 2 hours will usually suffice.

Always test the battery isolated or with all circuits off.

SPECIFIC GRAVITY

Specific gravity (SG) is a better way of testing the level of charge because it tells you the condition of each individual cell. Using a battery hydrometer, squeeze the bulb, insert the rubber tip into the cell, and slowly release the bulb to draw just enough electrolyte into the tube to float the glass float. Do not remove the tip from the cell. Where the surface of the liquid crosses the graduated scale in the float is the specific gravity of the electrolyte in this cell. When you have a reading, squeeze the bulb to return the electrolyte to the tested cell. Test each cell in turn.

As with voltage, SG measurements are most accurate if the battery has rested for 24 hours, but most stabilization takes place in the first few hours. If the battery has rested for 2 hours, the SG reading will be within about 0.005 of the 24-hour value.

In a healthy battery, cell-to-cell readings will be uniform. Over time some disparity can appear, which usually can be corrected by overcharging the battery. If the fully charged SG varies 50 points (0.050) between cells, replace the battery.

KEEP RECORDS

Charge new batteries, then check and log the specific gravity of each cell—after an appropriate rest—to establish the "full charge" mark. A record of future SG readings will track the condition of the battery and let you avoid unexpected failure.

CHAPTER 4

WIRE

Like a rode connects boat to anchor, every wire connects appliance to power source. The appropriate size for anchor chain depends on the anticipated load; likewise with the size of wire. And if you link chain to anchor with the wrong shackle, or you fail to safety-wire the pin, whose fault is it when the boat goes up on the rocks? In wiring, the same rules apply.

A wire could hardly find a more hostile environment than aboard a boat. To start with, there is a possibility—make that likelihood—that the wire will get wet. And even if it is never splashed or submerged, long-term exposure to moisture- and salt-laden sea air eventually has the same effect.

On a boat that gets use, the poor wire is always on watch, tossed around just like the rest of the crew. If long runs between attachment points let the wire flex with every dip and swoop, who can blame it when it succumbs to fatigue?

Then there is the problem of harmonics—the vibration that makes the cotter rings on your turnbuckles dance when the engine is running. A flexible wire just boogies to the beat, but if the wire is stiff or held captive, vibrations can cause it to work harden and fracture.

But the worst enemy of wire pressed into marine service is usually the installer. Either out of ignorance or parsimony, both yard workers and boatowners tend to choose wire too small for the job. They subject the wire to sharp edges, hot metal, and the crush at the bottom of lockers. They install the wrong terminals because that's what they have on hand. They entrust essential connections to a bargain-counter crimping tool.

No wonder electrical failures are common on boats, but they shouldn't be. All it takes to install wiring that will give decades of trouble-free service is the right wire, the right terminals, the right tools, and the right priority.

Every wire used aboard your boat needs to be the right type to withstand flexing and vibration, the right size to match current-carrying requirements, and appropriately insulated to resist moisture, petroleum products, and sunlight.

CONSTRUCTION

Boat wiring must be copper, but not all copper wiring is the same.

STRANDED

Never use solid wire on a boat, no matter how much you have left from a home wiring project. Wave- or motor-induced oscillations eventually fracture solid wire. Boat wiring must have the flexibility stranding provides. While boatbuilders may save a few dollars using type 2 wire, it is false economy for you to buy anything but type 3. Only type 3, the most flexible type, is appropriate for every use. A spool of type 3 aboard means always having the right wire at hand.

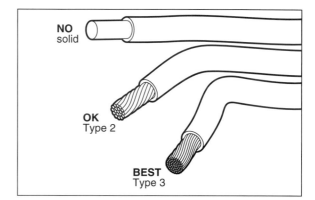

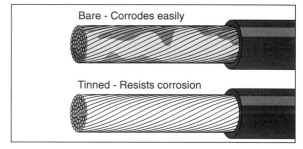

TINNED

Copper wire corrodes in the marine environment, reducing conductivity, especially at terminals and connections. Plating each strand with a thin coat of tin—called tinning—dramatically improves corrosion resistance. The additional cost of tinned wire is nominal, the benefits substantial. Under normal circumstances use only tinned wire.

DUPLEX

Stranded single-conductor wire is called hook-up or primary wire. Since most after-construction wiring requires two wires, duplex wire is more convenient and provides the added safety of a second layer of insulation. The best choice for most wiring projects is duplex safety wire, where the twin conductors are red (positive) and yellow (ground). Making the ground wire yellow rather than black reduces the chances of confusing a DC ground wire with an AC hot wire—also black.

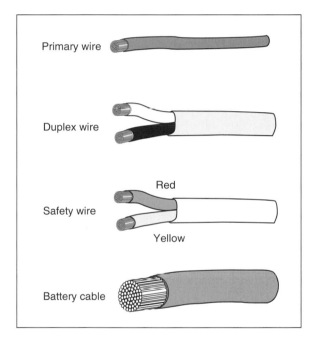

SIZE

As with water through a hose, electricity flows more easily through larger wire. It is essential to size wire for the maximum current flow you expect it to carry.

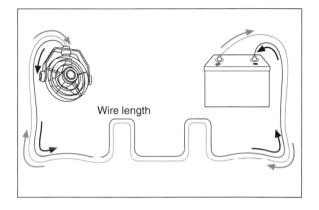

LENGTH

All sizing formulas and tables use wire length from the power source to the appliance(s) *and back to the power source.* Doubling the straight line distance to the battery is not adequate. You must determine the actual length of the wire by measuring along the path it will follow—up, over, and around. It is not unusual for a wire run to be more than twice the straight-line distance.

Each wire should be a single continuous run between terminals. Always cut wire a foot or two longer than your measurement. The obvious reason for this precaution is that you can easily shorten the wire after it is installed, but lengthening it requires a highly undesirable splice. Less obvious, "relaxed" wire is less likely to abrade or suffer from harmonic vibration than wire put under strain because it was cut a tad too short. A loop of extra wire (called a *service loop*) also facilitates maintenance.

•	18
•	16
•	14
●	12
●	10
●	8
●	6
●	4
●	2
●	1
●	0 (1/0)
●	00 (2/0)
●	000 (3/0)
●	0000 (4/0)

GAUGE

Electrical wire appropriate for marine use carries a gauge designation printed on the insulation. The smaller the gauge number, the larger the wire diameter. Aside from *that* cockeyed logic (life could be *so* much easier), wiring sold by marine outlets almost always carries an AWG (American Wire Gauge) rating, while the published selection tables—including those appearing here—are for SAE (Society of Automotive Engineers) rating. In the sizes you are likely to use, AWG wire is about 10% larger than SAE of the same gauge, so you are safe using the tables for either designation.

The minimum gauge for boat wiring is 16 AWG. An exception could be made for circuits drawing less than 1 amp, but remember that the smaller the wire, the more fragile it is, and fragile has no place on a boat.

CURRENT CAPACITY

The first step in wire sizing is determining how much current the wire must carry. A circuit with a single 25-watt light needs to carry only 2 amps (25 W / 12 V), but if six lights are on the circuit, the wiring must be capable of carrying at least 12 amps. Drawing more current through a wire than it can handle heats it up. How much heating a wire can tolerate before becoming a fire hazard depends on the insulation. The table shows the current capacity for various kinds of insulation.

From the table you can see that boat cable in the smallest recommended size—16 gauge—can safely carry 25 amps (21.3 amps inside an engine space because of the higher ambient temperature). Since few boat circuits exceed this, you generally need to consider current capacity only for charging circuits and when wiring high-draw equipment such as windlasses and inverters.

VOLTAGE DROP

Just because it isn't overloaded by current draw doesn't mean you can use 16-gauge wire for all your circuits. The smaller the wire, the greater its resistance—as the table at right shows—and voltage is used up pushing current through this resistance. Suppose, for example, the round-trip distance from the battery to a deckwash pump at the bow is 100 feet (30 m). The table shows that the resistance of 100 feet of 16-gauge wire will be 0.41 ohms, and we know from the pump specifications that the current draw is 10 amps. We can use Ohm's Law (V = IR) to find that it takes 4.1 volts (10A x 0.41Ω) just to get the current to the pump. This is called *voltage drop*. If the battery voltage is 12.6 volts and we lose 4.1 volts to resistance in the wire, we have only 8.5 volts at the pump—probably too little voltage to run it.

The formula allows you determine what size wire is required to deliver adequate voltage to the other end. CM is the circular mil area of the conductor, which allows you to enter the table to determine gauge. I is the current, L is the round-trip length of the wire, and 10.75 is the resistivity of copper. E is the allowable voltage drop, which is normally 0.36 volts—3% of lowest battery voltage. For the example pump, the formula gives us a CM value of 29,861. From the chart, we find that this is larger than 6 gauge, so the appropriate wire size is 4 gauge.

ALLOWABLE AMPERAGE

Wire Type	TW	THW, HWN, THWN	MTW, XHHW	AWM, BC5W2, UL1426 Boat Cable
Temperature Rating	60°C (140°F)	75°C (167°F)	90°C (194°F)	105°C (221°F)
Wire Gauge (AWG)	Outside/Inside Engine Space	Outside/Inside Engine Space	Outside/Inside Engine Space	Outside/Inside Engine Space
18	10 / 5.8	10 / 7.5	20 / 16.4	20 / 17.0
16	15 / 8.7	15 / 11.3	25 / 20.5	25 / 21.3
14	20 / 11.6	20 / 15.0	30 / 24.6	35 / 29.8
12	25 / 14.5	25 / 18.8	40 / 32.8	45 / 38.3
10	40 / 23.2	40 / 30.0	55 / 45.1	60 / 51.0
8	55 / 31.9	65 / 48.8	70 / 57.4	80 / 68.0
6	80 / 46.4	95 / 71.3	100 / 82.0	120 / 102
4	105 / 60.9	125 / 93.8	135 / 110	160 / 136
2	140 / 81.2	170 / 127	180 / 147	210 / 178
1	165 / 95.7	195 / 146	210 / 172	245 / 208
0	195 / 113	230 / 172	245 / 200	285 / 242
00	225 / 130	265 / 198	285 / 233	330 / 280
000	260 / 150	310 / 232	330 / 270	385 / 327
0000	300 / 174	380 / 270	385 / 315	445 / 378

WIRE SIZE FORMULA

$$CM = \frac{I \times L \times 10.75}{E}$$

CM	=	Wire size in circular mils
I	=	Current
L	=	Length of wire (round trip)
E	=	Allowable voltage drop—generally 0.36

KEY TO WIRE CODES

BC	=	Boat cable
H	=	Heat resistant (75°C rating)
HH	=	High heat resistant (90°C rating)
N	=	Nylon jacket
M	=	Oil resistant
T	=	Thermoplastic
W	=	Moisture resistant
X	=	Cross-linked polymer

WIRE RESISTANCE

Circular Mils (CM)	Wire Gauge (AWG)	Ohms per 100 Feet (@ 77°F)
1,620	18	.654
2,580	16	.409
4,110	14	.258
6,530	12	.162
10,380	10	.102
16,510	8	.064
26,240	6	.040
41,740	4	.025
66,360	2	.016
83,690	1	.013
105,600	0	.010
133,100	00	.008
167,800	000	.006
211,600	0000	.005

Note: Circular mils are calculated by squaring the wire diameter in mils (thousandths of an inch)

10% DROP

MOST TEXTS also provide a 10% drop table, but a drop greater than 3% is not allowed (by American Boat and Yacht Council standards) for essential electrical items such as bilge blowers, running lights, and navigation equipment. While some items, such as cabin lights, can tolerate lower voltage, it is almost never a good idea to use the smaller-gauge wire. The cost savings is inconsequential compared to the potential problems inadequate wiring can spawn. Reduced weight is a desirable bene-fit for wiring leading to the masthead, but aside from the essential nature of most mast-mounted electrics, mast wiring also receives the most punishment—a poor argument for using less robust wire.

3% TABLE

I find the formula easier to use, but you may prefer using this table to deter-mine appropriate wire size. Use the current draw to select the row, the round-trip wire length to select the column. The number where these two intersect is the recommended wire gauge.

	ROUND-TRIP LENGTH OF CONDUCTOR (FEET)								
Current (Amps)	10	20	30	40	60	80	100	120	140
			Minimum Wire Size (AWG)						
1	16*	16*	16*	16*	16	14	14	14	12
2	16*	16*	16	14	14	12	10	10	8
5	16*	14	12	10	10	8	6	6	6
10	14	10	10	8	6	6	4	4	2
15	12	10	8	6	6	4	2	2	1
20	10	8	6	6	4	2	2	1	0
25	10	6	6	4	2	2	1	0	2/0
30	10	6	4	4	2	1	0	2/0	3/0
40	8	6	4	2	1	0	2/0	3/0	4/0
50	6	4	2	2	0	2/0	3/0	4/0	
60	6	4	2	1	2/0	3/0	4/0		
70	6	2	1	0	3/0	4/0			
80	6	2	1	0	3/0	4/0			
90	4	2	0	2/0	4/0				
100	4	2	0	2/0	4/0				

*18-gauge wire has adequate current capacity but is too fragile for boat use.

24 VOLTS

LARGER BOATS AND MULTIHULLS, because of long wire runs, may find it advantageous to adopt a 24-volt system. Our 120-watt (10A x 12V) deckwash pump in the previous example (page 46) would draw only 5 amps in a 24-volt version (120W / 24V). Also, a 3% volt-age drop in a 24-volt system is 0.72 volts. Using these new values in the voltage drop formula, CM = 5A x 100' x 10.75 / 0.72V, or 7,465. From the chart, we find that 10 gauge wire has a CM of 9,343, more than enough to handle this load. Aside from the significant differ-ence in size and weight, smaller wires are far easier to work with. Purchasing 100 feet (30 m) of 10 AWG wire rather than 4 AWG also results in a cost savings of more than $150 for this circuit alone!

INSULATION

Insulation prevents unwanted contact between the wire and other components of the boat—including crew. It also protects the wire from the elements.

DESIGNATION

Wire appropriate for boat use will have a designation code printed on the insulation or jacket. The keys shown here let you interpret most common codes. For example, THWN has thermoplastic insulation, a heat rating of 75°C, is suitable for wet locations, and it has an abrasion-resistant nylon jacket. XHHW designates a wire with a crossed-linked polymer insulation (stronger than PVC), a high heat rating of 90°C, and suitable for wet locations.

    The break-down voltage of the insulation—typically 600 volts—should also be printed on the wire jacket, along with the gauge of the enclosed conductor.

KEY TO WIRE CODES		
BC	=	Boat cable
H	=	Heat resistant (75°C rating)
HH	=	High heat resistant (90°C rating)
N	=	Nylon jacket
M	=	Oil resistant
T	=	Thermoplastic
W	=	Moisture resistant
X	=	Cross-linked polymer

BOAT CABLE

In recent years wire meeting stringent standards set by Underwriters Laboratories—called UL 1426—has become widely available to boatowners. Specifically designed for the marine environment, this wire is known as boat cable. Typical jacket designation is BC5W2, where the two numbers designate dry and wet environment heat ratings respectively. It is type 3 for maximum flexibility, and while not specified in the standard, the best boat cable has each strand tinned for maximum corrosion resistance. When available, tinned boat cable from a reputable supplier is your best choice for all wiring needs.

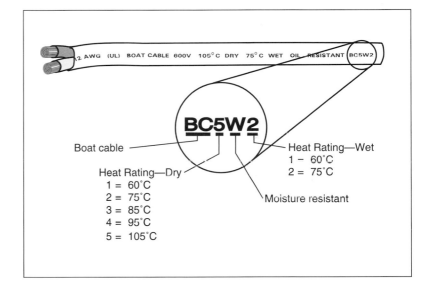

12 AWG (UL) BOAT CABLE 600V 105°C DRY 75°C WET OIL RESISTANT BC5W2

BC5W2

Boat cable

Heat Rating—Dry
1 = 60°C
2 = 75°C
3 = 85°C
4 = 95°C
5 = 105°C

Heat Rating—Wet
1 = 60°C
2 = 75°C

Moisture resistant

COLOR

This chart is included mostly for reference. While color coding is nice, it is rarely practical. However, you should use red wires for DC positive conductors only, and make all DC negative conductors yellow. Existing negative leads on your boat are likely to be black, but as previously mentioned, yellow has replaced black as the standard to distinguish DC negative conductors from the hot side of AC circuits.

ABYC RECOMMENDED WIRING COLORS	
COLOR	**USE**
Red	General DC positive conductor
Yellow	Preferred DC negative conductor
Black	Alternative DC negative conductor
Green or green with yellow stripe	General DC grounding conductor
Dark blue	Cabin and instrument lights
Dark Gray	Navigation lights, tachometer
Brown	Pumps, alternator charge light
Brown with yellow stripe	Bilge blower
Orange	Accessory feed
Purple	Ignition, instrument feed
Yellow with red stripe	Starting circuit
Light blue	Oil pressure
Tan	Water temperature
Pink	Fuel gauge

ROUTING

Attempts to wire a new circuit sometimes reveal unanticipated barriers to a suitable route for the wire. It is prudent to run the wiring before you mount a new electrical item in case routing realities dictate an alternative location.

HIGH AND DRY

Wire and water is always a bad combination. Route wires as far above the bilge as possible. Dead space under side decks is ideal.

RACEWAYS

Running wire inside raceways has the dual benefits of protecting the wire and giving continuous support (for horizontal runs). Wooden raceways can masquerade as cabin trim.

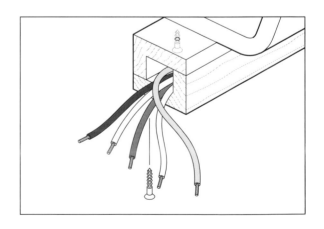

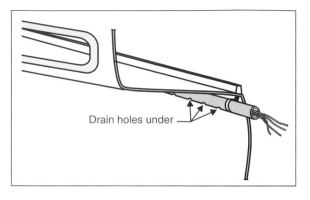

Drain holes under

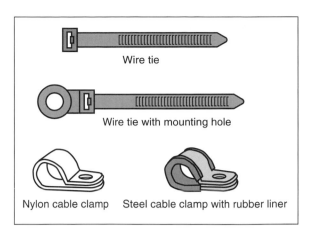

Wire tie

Wire tie with mounting hole

Nylon cable clamp   Steel cable clamp with rubber liner

CONDUIT

Rigid PVC conduit makes perfect lightweight raceways for out-of-view locations. Mount conduit under the side deck or as high as possible in locker spaces. Drill drain holes in low spots (before the wire is installed!) to prevent the conduit from trapping water. Do not use PVC conduit in engine spaces.

SUPPORT

Wires not continuously supported in raceways must be supported at least every 18 inches (45 cm). Cable clamps and wire ties simplify this requirement. Use metal clamps where loss of support could result in a hazard.

Leather

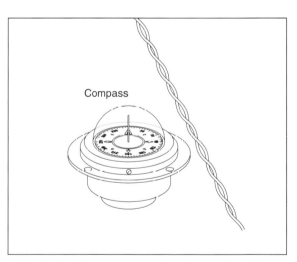

Compass

GROMMETS

Where wires pass through holes in panel boxes, masts, bulkheads, and other components, the hole must be lined to protect the wire from chafe.

TWISTED PAIRS

Direct current flowing through a wire produces a magnetic field that can interfere with the compass. Twisting positive and negative leads causes opposing fields to cancel. All wiring (other than coax) within 2 feet (0.6 m) of the steering or autopilot compass must be twisted in pairs.

CONNECTIONS

Other than chafe or lying against hot metal, wires rarely experience failures in the middle of a wire run. Almost all wiring problems occur at the terminal connections.

CRIMP CONNECTORS

You will minimize wiring problems if you terminate all wire ends with a crimp connector.

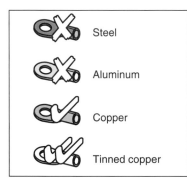

Steel

Aluminum

Copper

Tinned copper

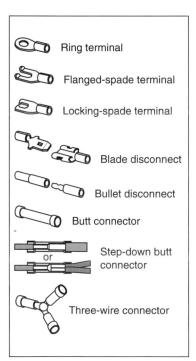

Ring terminal

Flanged-spade terminal

Locking-spade terminal

Blade disconnect

Bullet disconnect

Butt connector

Step-down butt connector

Three-wire connector

MATERIAL

Terminals used on a boat must always be copper, never steel or aluminum. Terminals should be tin-plated to resist corrosion.

SIZE

Selecting the proper connector requires that you match it to the wire gauge *and* to the size of the terminal screw.

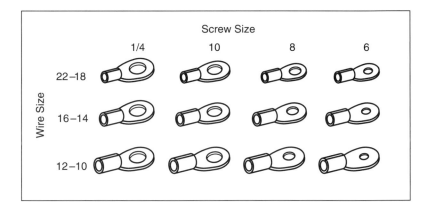

TYPE

Ring terminals are the best choice for all connectors unless the terminal screw is captive. In that case, use flanged spade connectors. Use butt connectors for appliances supplied with wire leads instead of terminals. Step-down butt connectors let you connect heavy supply wires to lighter leads. To simplify servicing, it can be a good idea to make the connection with blade or snap connectors instead of butt connectors. Three-way connectors are useful for tapping into an existing circuit.

CRIMPING

You simply cannot make dependable crimp connections with a rigging knife and a pair of pliers. Plan to add a wire stripper and a good-quality crimper to your tool collection.

STRIPPING

Remove only enough insulation for the wire to reach the end of the barrel of the terminal. Because SAE wire is smaller, most hardware store and auto supply wire strippers will cut into AWG wire. Nicks in the wire lead to corrosion, especially on a boat. Using the hole labeled for larger wire works for some sizes but is less satisfactory than buying a stripper for AWG wire.

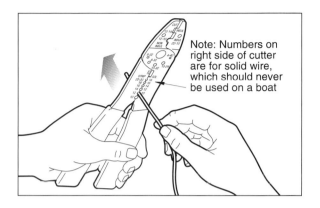

Note: Numbers on right side of cutter are for solid wire, which should never be used on a boat

MAKING THE CRIMP

Grip the terminal in the correct die in the crimper, fully insert the wire into the terminal, and squeeze. If the barrel has a seam, the crimp indent should be opposite.

In the hands of an amateur, only a ratchet crimper will give consistent crimps. Unfortunately, ratchet crimpers are far easier to use on a workbench than in the awkward work positions boat wiring can require. Many find the less-expensive pliers-style crimper better suited for onboard wiring. With practice you can make perfect crimps with a pliers-style crimper.

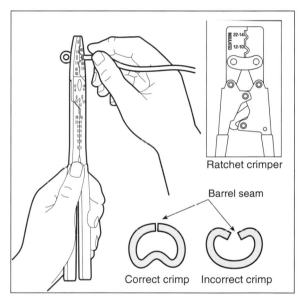

Ratchet crimper

Barrel seam

Correct crimp   Incorrect crimp

DOUBLE CRIMP

Better terminals feature a brass sleeve that can be crimped over the insulated wire to add mechanical strength. This type of terminal is usually installed with a double crimp tool.

Second crimp grips insulation

PULL

There is only one accepted field test for a crimp terminal—pull on it. Test *every* crimp terminal this way. Without using any tool, grip the terminal and the wire and try to separate them. If they come apart, the crimp was bad.

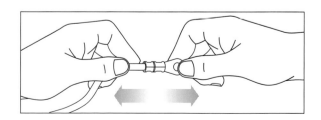

SOLDERING

If you use tinned wire and tinned terminals, most experts agree that soldering is not required. However, if you do it well, soldering improves the electrical connection between wire and terminal, especially as the connection ages. The potential for circuit-breaking corrosion makes soldering essential if either the wire or the terminal is untinned.

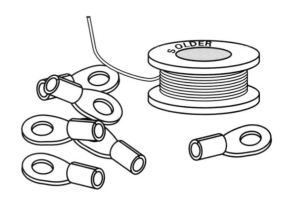

UNINSULATED TERMINALS

If you want to solder, use uninsulated terminals. Crimp the terminal to the stripped wire before soldering. Never depend on solder to provide the mechanical connection; a faulty connection can generate enough heat to melt the solder and let the wire drop out of the terminal.

ALUMINUM-CAN HEAT SINK

Melting the wire's insulation releases chemicals that are corrosive to the wire. To avoid this, slip a split 2-inch (5 cm) disk cut from an aluminum can over the bare wire where it enters the terminal to dissipate the heat before it reaches the insulation.

TINNING THE SOLDERING IRON

A SOLDERING IRON will not heat the joint properly unless it is properly tinned. Start by cleaning the tip of the cold iron with emery cloth to remove old flux and solder. Next, heat the tip and dip it in soldering paste. Coat the tip with solder, then wipe off the excess with a damp cloth. The hot tip should be completely silvered and shiny.

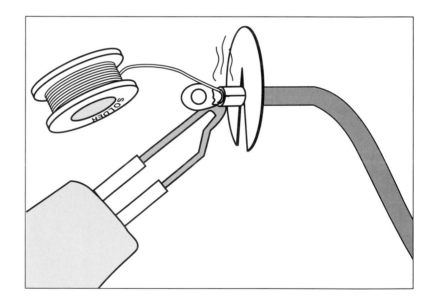

HEAT THE WIRE

Heat the barrel of the terminal with a well-tinned soldering iron until solder touched to the ends of the wire melts. Keeping the tip against the terminal, flow enough solder into the wire to just fill the barrel. Withdraw the solder and the heat and leave the joint undisturbed for a minute. A proper joint will be smooth and shiny, not dull or lumpy.

SOLDERED = SOLID

The only drawback to soldering crimp terminals—other than the effort it requires—is that the solder in effect converts the stranded wire to solid. This is of no consequence unless the solder wicks beyond the barrel of the terminal, where it causes a hard spot that can be susceptible to fracturing from vibration. Use a heat-shield at the barrel entrance and limit the amount of solder to avoid this problem.

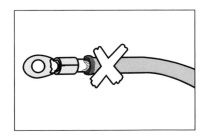

HEAT-SHRINK

Unlike electrical tape, which too often falls off or becomes a gooey mess, heat-shrink tubing is as durable as the insulation on the wire. Heat-shrink is often touted as waterproof, of dubious value except for butt connectors (which can be entirely enclosed). The real value of heat shrink is to provide reliable insulation. If the heat-shrink is adhesive lined, it also relieves some of the strain on the wire connection.

Slide heat-shrink tubing onto the wire before installing connectors. If a connector will be soldered, be sure the tubing is far enough from the end to remain cool. After the joint is crimped (and soldered), slide the tubing over it and heat the tubing by playing a flame under it, or shrink it with a heat gun.

BARE WIRES

Wrapping a bare wire around a terminal screw damages the wire when the screw is tightened. This type of electrical connection should be avoided. Set-screws are also damaging when they bear directly on the wire. Twisted-bare-wire connections don't damage the wire, but lack the tight contact and strain resistance of crimp connections. If you find yourself without an alternative, soldering a twisted-wire connection perfects the electrical connection, and if the joint is well sealed in heat-shrink tubing, it should be trouble-free.

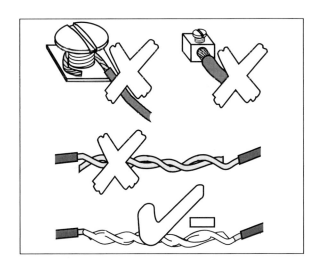

WIRE NUTS

Wire nuts are NEVER an acceptable means of making electrical connections on a boat.

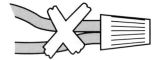

OVERLOAD PROTECTION

Excess current can turn a wire into a heating element capable of igniting anything flammable. Any wire aboard that is not overload protected represents a grave and unacceptable danger to boat and crew.

FUSES

The principle behind a fuse is simple; too much current melts the conductor and opens the circuit. Fuses are cheap, foolproof, and less convenient than breakers only when they blow—which will be almost never if the wiring is done well.

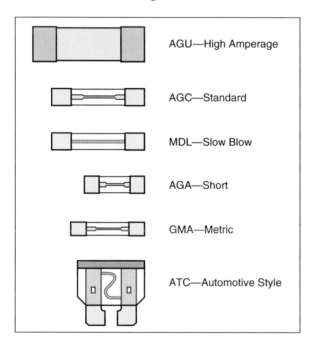

AGU—High Amperage

AGC—Standard

MDL—Slow Blow

AGA—Short

GMA—Metric

ATC—Automotive Style

CIRCUIT BREAKERS

Circuit breakers don't protect a circuit any better than a fuse, but since breakers can be reset over and over, they do simplify troubleshooting the faulty circuit. Breakers also do double duty as a switch to de-energize the circuit.

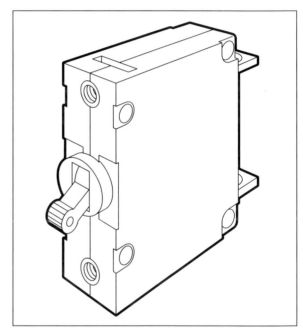

SIZING

The size of the fuse or breaker is determined by the sum of all the loads on the circuit OR by the current-carrying capacity of the smallest wire in the circuit, *whichever is smaller.* For example, 12-AWG boat cable to the masthead tricolor is adequately protected by a 50-amp breaker—marine standards allow the breaker threshold to be up to 150% of the wire rating (45 amps for 12 AWG). But since the normal load on this circuit should never exceed 2 amps, a 5-amp breaker will detect a problem sooner.

INSTALLING

Fuses and breakers are always installed in series in the positive conductor of a circuit. Locate them as close to the power source as possible. In practice, they are typically installed in a panel board located near the batteries.

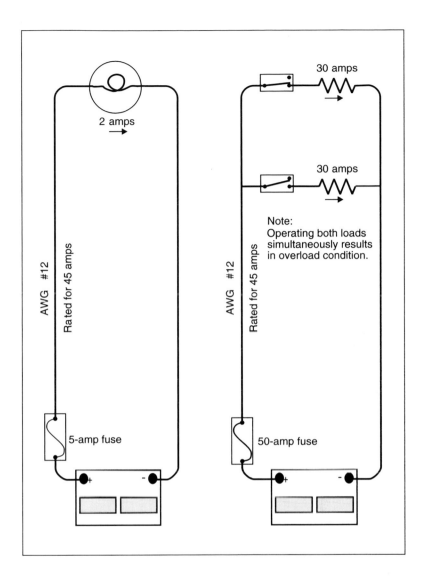

2 amps

30 amps

30 amps

Note:
Operating both loads simultaneously results in overload condition.

AWG #12
Rated for 45 amps

AWG #12
Rated for 45 amps

5-amp fuse

50-amp fuse

SUPPLY SIDE

Hundreds of thousands of boats have been wired with no overload protection for the supply cable to the electrical panel, and more than a few of those boats have been destroyed by a resulting fire. Today high-amperage fuses and/or breakers capable of carrying starter loads are available at nominal cost. The main positive cable from the battery should be overload protected *at the battery*, and the main lead from the battery selector switch to the distribution panel should also be protected. Also make sure the wiring to the engine panel is fuse-protected. If you do not have these safeguards, they are the first modifications you should make to your electrical system.

Size any fuse in the starting circuit as large as the capacity of the cable allows; you want protection from a dead short, but you do not want the fuse to interfere with starting the engine. In the feeder line to the distribution panel, the size of the fuse or breaker must not exceed the rated capacity of the feeder wire or the load capacity of the panel.

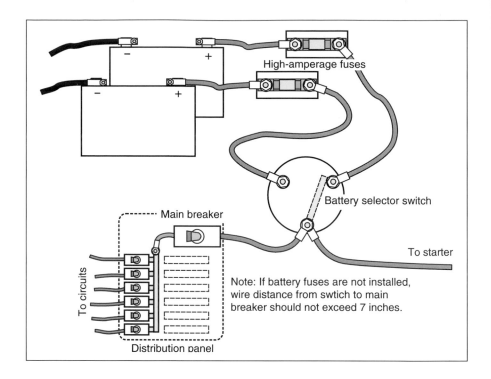

High-amperage fuses

Battery selector switch

To starter

Main breaker

To circuits

Note: If battery fuses are not installed, wire distance from swtich to main breaker should not exceed 7 inches.

Distribution panel

EQUIPMENT PROTECTION

The breakers in the panel are to protect the wiring from overload. Protecting an individual piece of equipment requires an additional fuse, either built in to the equipment or series installed in the positive lead with an in-line holder or a fuse block.

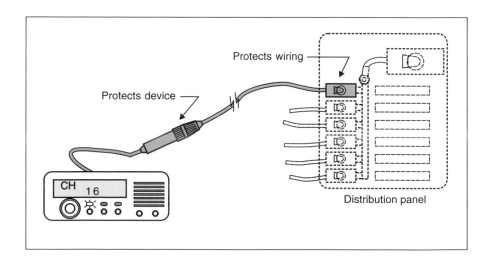

Protects wiring

Protects device

CH 16

Distribution panel

SWITCHES

Switches allow you to interrupt the flow of current. Like fuses and breakers, switches are installed in series in the positive conductor.

SPST

The simple ON/OFF switch is a single pole, single throw (SPST) switch. The switch has two terminals that are connected in the ON position, not connected in the OFF position.

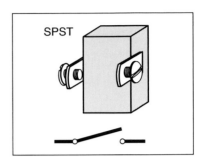

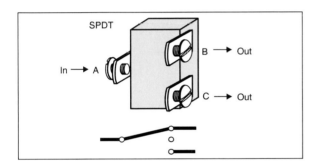

DT

Three terminals usually indicates a double-throw (DT) switch. Moving the toggle in one direction connects terminals A and B. "Throwing" the toggle the other way connects A and C. In the middle position, none of the terminals are connected.

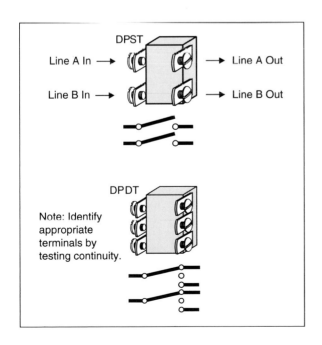

DP

Double-pole (DP) switches let you connect and disconnect two conductors simultaneously. Installed in both the positive and negative sides of a circuit, a DP switch completely isolates all components beyond the switch. Although double-pole breakers are rarely seen in 12-volt circuits, they are superior to single-pole breakers because they completely disconnect the circuit rather than just open it.

Double pole switches can also be double throw (DPDT).

BATTERY SELECTOR

The typical battery selector is a rotary switch allowing the boat's electrical system to be connected to battery 1, both batteries, battery 2, or disconnected from any power source. A better alternative is detailed in Chapter 7.

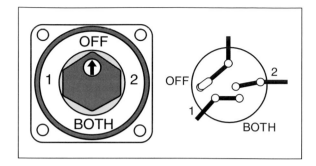

NEATNESS COUNTS

After using the right components and making good connections, the third essential to a trouble-free electrical system is neatness.

LABELING

It is just common sense to label both ends of a wire run, yet this step is often overlooked. The consequence is wasted time later when you need to work on this circuit. In an emergency, the absence of labeling can be dangerous.

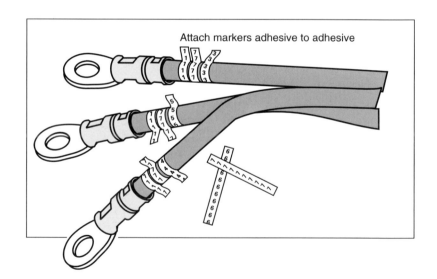

Attach markers adhesive to adhesive

WIRE MARKERS

Electrical suppliers sell books, sheets, or rolls of adhesive wire markers that are easily applied to the insulation near the terminals at each end. You can simply give the wire a number, which you will record on a drawing of your boat's wiring (see Chapter 6), or you can use a code, for example, "GL" for galley lights.

CLEAR SHRINK TUBING

Covering wire markers with clear shrink tubing ensures that they will never come unglued. You can also write your own markers on paper and capture it with shrink tubing. Labels written on tape flags are better than nothing, but tape soon falls off in the wet environment of a boat.

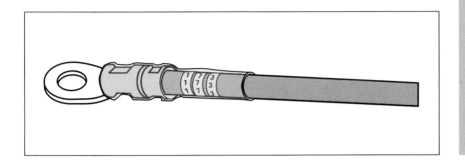

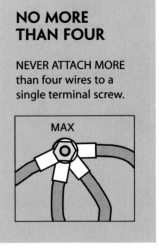

NO MORE THAN FOUR

NEVER ATTACH MORE than four wires to a single terminal screw.

MAX

TERMINAL STRIPS

Terminal strips are superior to three-way connectors for wiring several appliances to the same circuit. A terminal strip/fuse block combination allows you to protect each appliance independently and have all fuses in an accessible location. Set-screw style terminals should have an internal shoe to keep the end of the screw from damaging the wire.

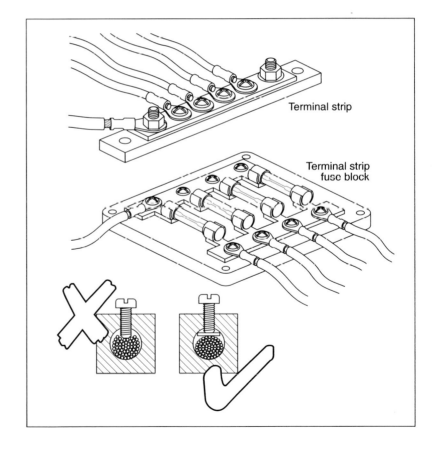

Terminal strip

Terminal strip fuse block

JUNCTION BOXES

Terminal strips and fuse blocks need to be protected with a cover or by installing them in junction boxes.

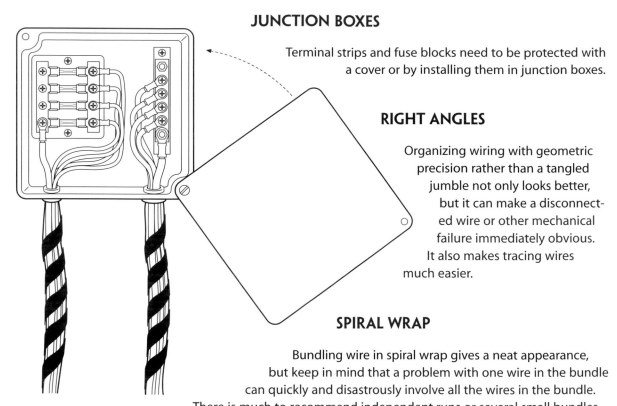

RIGHT ANGLES

Organizing wiring with geometric precision rather than a tangled jumble not only looks better, but it can make a disconnected wire or other mechanical failure immediately obvious. It also makes tracing wires much easier.

SPIRAL WRAP

Bundling wire in spiral wrap gives a neat appearance, but keep in mind that a problem with one wire in the bundle can quickly and disastrously involve all the wires in the bundle. There is much to recommend independent runs or several small bundles rather than a harness containing every wire running fore and aft. AC and DC conductors must never be bundled together.

PANEL LOCATION

Factory-installed electrical panels, particularly in older and/or smaller boats, are too often installed beneath the companionway and/or through the engine-compartment bulkhead. Wiring should not lead through the engine compartment unless it is engine wiring, and the electrical panel should be mounted where a dousing with rain, spray, or green water will be unlikely.

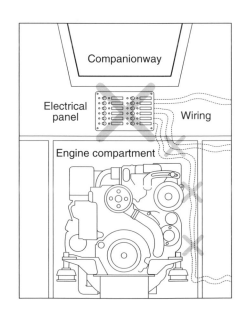

Antenna connections on a boat must be made with a special kind of cable that incorporates a surrounding wire braid. This is called coaxial cable, or simply coax. The signal travels on the outside of the core conductor and the inside of the braid, essentially trapped inside the cable.

SIZE

Bigger is better—period. Anything other than RG-213/U or RG-8/U will cut your transmitting power *at the antenna* by about 1% per foot—costly economy to save a few bucks on cable. For short runs, you might use RG-8X, called mini 8. Never use RG-58/U. And never use TV coax, no matter how big it is; it has incorrect impedance for marine radio use.

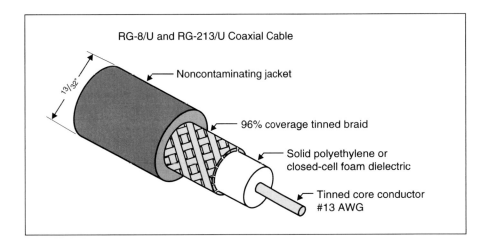

RG-8/U and RG-213/U Coaxial Cable

Noncontaminating jacket

96% coverage tinned braid

Solid polyethylene or closed-cell foam dielectric

Tinned core conductor #13 AWG

CONSTRUCTION

Both RG-213/U and RG-8/U are the same size, but the more durable jacket on RG-213/U gives a life expectancy of 20 years or more. For marine use the jacket should carry the "noncontaminating" designation. As with electrical wiring, tinned conductors—both the core and the braid—make the coax much more resistant to corrosion. To avoid signal leakage, the braid should be tightly woven, providing at least 96% shielding. A foam dielectric reduces power losses, but a solid polyethylene dielectric is better for marine use unless you are sure the foam is closed cell.

CONNECTIONS

Crimp-on connectors rarely last more than a couple of years before resistance caused by internal corrosion degrades radio performance. All coax connectors need to be soldered. The connector for both RG-213/U and RG-8/U is designated PL-259, and the same connector goes on both ends of the cable.

Manicure scissors are perfect for cleanly trimming the braid.

Cut end square and remove $1\frac{1}{8}$" of jacket without nicking braid.

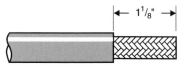

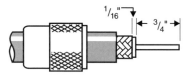

Bare $\frac{3}{4}$" of center core, taking care not to nick it. Trim braid back $\frac{1}{16}$" and tin it. Slide coupling ring onto cable.

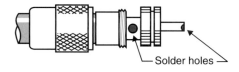

Screw plug assembly onto cable and solder it sparingly to both core and braid through solder holes. Screw coupling ring to plug assembly. Touch ohmmeter probes to center contact and plug body to check for short.

Solder holes

WEATHERPROOFING

Join two PL-259 connectors by threading them onto a barrel connector, called a PL-258. To avoid moisture intrusion, this entire assembly must be encased in adhesive-lined heat-shrink tubing. A drip loop will prevent guttering.

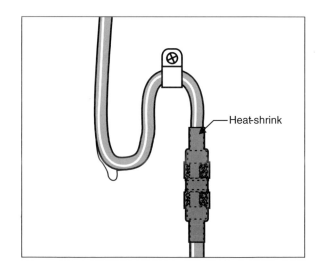

Heat-shrink

BACKSTAY CONNECTION

An insulated backstay often doubles as the SSB or ham radio antenna. Note that on a fiberglass boat, a lower insulator is unnecessary as long as the backstay chain plate is not bonded to the boat's grounding system. During transmission, the energized antenna can burn you, so insulate the bottom 6 feet (1.8 m) of the stay with rubber hose.

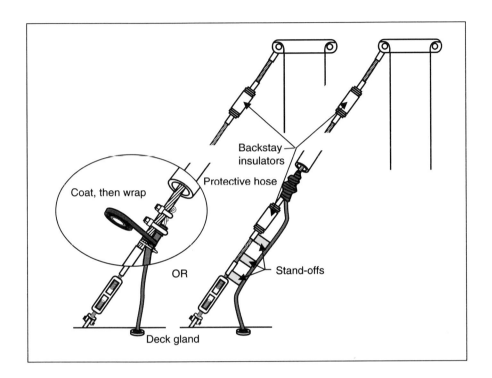

Coat, then wrap

Backstay insulators

Protective hose

OR

Stand-offs

Deck gland

The connection to the stay is made as shown, using stainless steel cable clamps. The wire is typically antenna lead-in, held clear of the stay with stand-offs (as shown), but if you elect to use coax instead, be sure only the center conductor is in contact with the stay, not the braid. The entire connection should be protected from the weather by coating it with electrician's putty (Coax Seal), then wrapping it *from bottom to top* with self-amalgamating tape.

COPPER RIBBON

Ground connections for high-frequency radios—SSB and ham—should be made with copper foil ribbon rather than wire. Radio frequency (RF) current travels on the surface of the conductor, so the more surface, the better the ground connection. That directly translates into longer-range, clearer radio transmission.

Three-inch-wide (7.6 cm) copper foil is a good choice for RF grounding. The thickness of the foil is not important other than for durability. We take a closer look at how to make a good RF ground connection in Chapter 9.

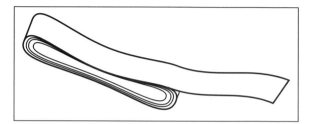

CHAPTER 5
CIRCUITS

B ack in Chapter 2 we defined circuit as a configuration of electrically connected components. For a circuit to allow the flow of electricity, it must be *closed*, i.e., one end of the circuit must be connected to the positive side of the power source and the other to the negative side. Any break in continuity *opens* the circuit and interrupts the flow of current.

Circuits can be as simple (and spectacular) as a steel wrench across battery terminals—called a *short circuit*—or as complex as the innards of a super computer. The electrical circuits found on pleasure boats are at the simple end of this spectrum.

Circuits are like the petals of a penciled daisy, each a loop starting and ending at the flower's center. Aboard a boat, the center of this electrical bloom is the distribution panel.

The various circuits on a boat are not identical. One may feed a single pump, while another branches through several lights. One may include fuses and switches and diodes, while another is protected and regulated only by the panel breaker. One circuit may require 6 gauge wire while 16 gauge is adequate for another. But despite such differences, all supply circuits on a boat are similar enough that understanding one circuit is tantamount to understanding them all.

WIRING DIAGRAMS

Circuits are easier to understand when we draw them.
A diagram of how the various
components are connected is
called a schematic. It works
much like a map, with electrical
components substituting for
towns and wire for roads.
Schematics don't just help you
visualize the circuit; they show
where to look and—just as valuable—where *not* to look when
the current traveling these wires
suffers a breakdown.

SYMBOLS

Labeled boxes or circles can represent the various components, but a
handful of symbols makes circuit diagrams easier to draw and easier
to read. Electrical symbols are not entirely standardized, so you may
encounter alternative representations of the same component.

CONDUCTOR

The solid lines on a schematic represent
the wire (or sometimes copper ribbon or
copper terminal strips) that connect the
various components.

TERMINAL OR CONNECTION

A dot or small circle indicates a connection. When lines cross without a dot,
the represented wires are not connected. Sometimes a hump is used at line
intersections to make it clear that no junction is indicated, but this adds unnecessary complexity.

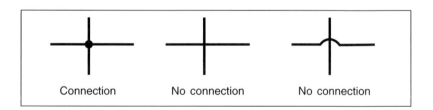

BATTERY

For 12-volt circuits, the battery is both the beginning and the end of the circuit. Use the battery symbol or a pair of terminal symbols marked with a +
and a −.

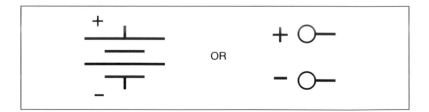

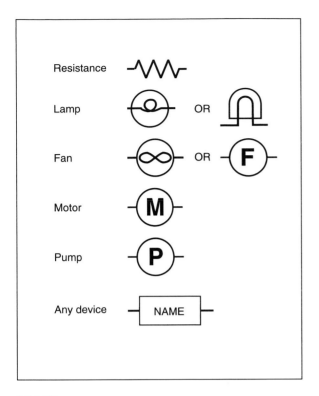

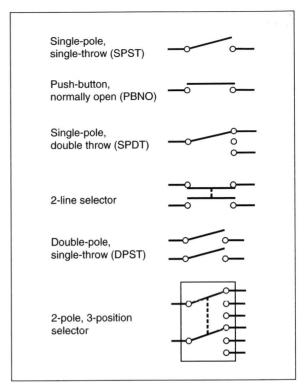

LOADS

You can show all loads with the zigzag resistance symbol, but schematics tell more at a glance if the symbol is more specific.

SWITCHES

The simplest switch symbol depicts a hinged conductor between two terminals. The symbols for specialized or more complicated switches are equally intuitive.

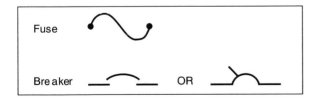

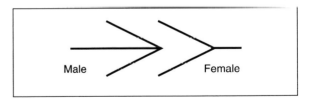

FUSES AND BREAKERS

You can use the fuse symbol for all load-protection devices, or distinguish between fuses and breakers.

CONNECTOR

For ease of servicing, it is often a good idea to use pull-apart plugs to connect an appliance to the power circuit.

MORE ABOUT GROUND

WIRING DIAGRAMS for automobiles often show a ground symbol on the negative side of loads rather than a return wire because cars use a single-wire system, grounding the negative side of loads to the chassis. Proper boat wiring is a two-wire system—called insulated return—with the negative side of the load ultimately connected to the negative terminal of the battery (or other power source). A ground symbol appears on a boat wiring diagram only where the negative terminal of the battery is grounded, usually by connecting it to the engine and thus to the water through the shaft and prop. Typically the alternator is similarly grounded, as are engine-mounted electrics that use the engine for the return side of the circuit.

On a boat, the ground symbol is used more often in diagrams of bonding systems intended to reduce corrosion and/or reduce the potential for lightning-strike damage (see Chapter 9). Some electronics, particularly high-frequency radios, also require a connection to ground.

GROUND

The ground symbol indicates a connection to earth—in the case of a boat, a connection to the water the boat is floating in, usually through engine, shaft, and prop or through an externally mounted (and submerged) grounding plate.

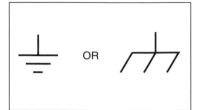

DIODES

Diodes are primarily used as check valves, passing current one way, but blocking the flow the other way. Light-emitting diodes (LEDs) are used today for almost all panel lights. Because of their astoundingly low current draw, LEDs are on their way to replacing 12-volt incandescent lamps.

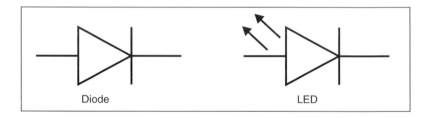

Diode   LED

ALTERNATOR

The engine-driven alternator is the main source of charging current on most boats. A generator performs the same function.

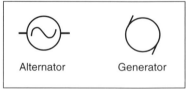

Alternator   Generator

METERS

Smart sailors are more and more including integral meters in various circuits to show immediate current flow or voltage level.

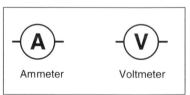

Ammeter   Voltmeter

A circuit requires only three components: a power source, a load, and conductors connecting the two.

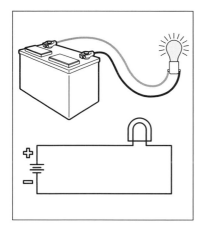

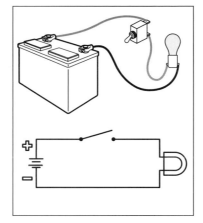

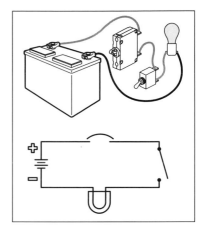

CLOSED CIRCUIT

Connecting the wire leads from a lamp to the terminals of a battery closes the circuit and, if the battery has a charge, illuminates the light.

OPEN CIRCUIT

We can stop the flow of current by disconnecting one of the wires, but adding a switch to the circuit makes extinguishing the light more convenient. Switches are always installed in the positive side of the circuit.

OVERLOAD PROTECTION

To avoid the dangers of a short, every circuit must also include a fuse or breaker in the positive side, as close to the power source as possible.

SERIES

Controlling components like switches, fuses, and diodes are always wired in series with the load.

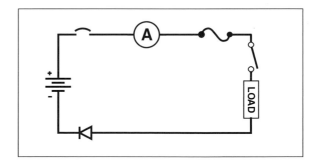

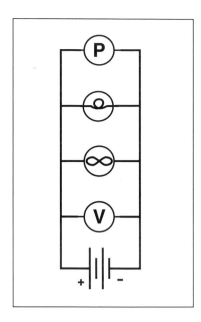

PARALLEL

When a circuit supplies more than one load, the loads are almost always connected in parallel. Parallel circuits all enjoy the same voltage.

REAL WORLD

A typical real-world circuit may have both series and parallel components, and some *branches* of the circuit may be open concurrent with others being closed.

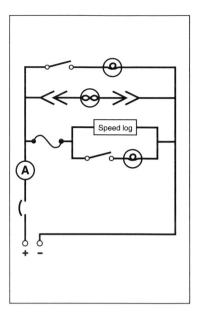

MAPPING YOUR OWN BOAT

Few boats are provided with factory schematics. Taking a few hours to work up a diagram of the wiring of your boat will pay sizable dividends: an accurate wiring diagram makes electrical problems much easier to diagnose; the process of tracing the wiring will familiarize you with your boat's all-important and otherwise-hidden electrical system, and will serve as an electrical survey to uncover shortcomings and potential problems; and the hands-on experience is sure to bolster your confidence as an electrician.

AC CAUTION

Before you start tracing wires, be sure that your boat is disconnected from shore power, and DISCONNECT YOUR INVERTER FROM THE BATTERY. It is far too easy to confuse 12-volt wiring with 120-volt wiring, and if the AC system is energized, such a mistake could be deadly.

Mapping AC wiring is a good idea, often leading to the discovery of serious deficiencies such as exposed connections, the absence of an AC circuit breaker, or reversed polarity. If you want to map your boat's AC system now while you are tracing the 12-volt system, read Chapter 8 first so you will know what kinds of problems you should be watching for.

WYSIWYG

The best way to create a wiring diagram is to start with a layout of your boat and draw in every appliance, outlet, and remote switch more or less where they are actually located. This is usually an eye-opener as to how many electrical items are aboard.

The larger the sheet of paper, the less congested this drawing will become. Labeled boxes and circles will be adequate symbols.

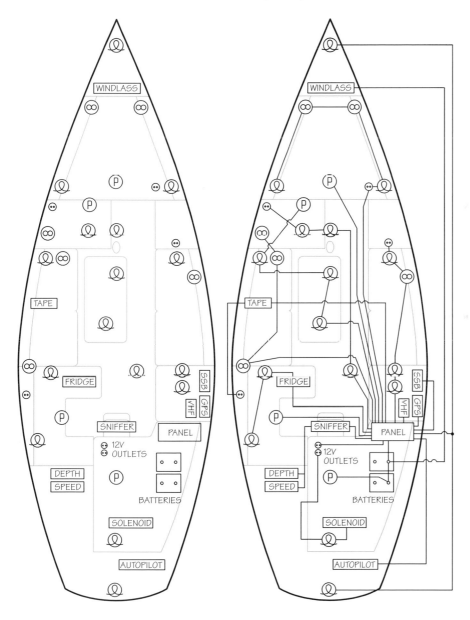

Once you have all the components on the drawing, convert it to a single-line wiring diagram by connecting the items on each circuit. With everything switched on, you can identify which items are on the same circuit by throwing the breaker and observing what goes off. Some circuits may not originate at the breaker panel; automatic bilge pumps, for example, are often connected directly to the battery so they will remain operational even with the main battery switch off.

The point of this step is to establish which components are interconnected. If you end up with some components on your drawing unconnected, just leave them for the moment. When you start tracing wiring, how they are connected into the system will become clear.

CIRCUIT DIAGRAMS

The basic sailboat electrical system typically has a main circuit—connecting the batteries to both the starter and the distribution panel—and at least six (usually more) branch circuits supplying power to lights, pumps, and other electrical items. In addition, there are charging circuits, which we haven't yet covered (Chapter 7), but which you can still diagram; and dedicated circuits connected directly to the battery for such items as bilge pumps and SSB radios.

Diagramming circuits will be easier if you do each circuit on a separate page. Where a wire is identified by a label, a color, or even the printed designation on the jacket, noting this information on your drawing can help you find the other end. Note, however, that factory "electricians" are notorious for grabbing any color available when the last spool empties, so a wire that leaves the panel blue might be pink when it reaches the appliance, perhaps with a butt splice behind the headliner.

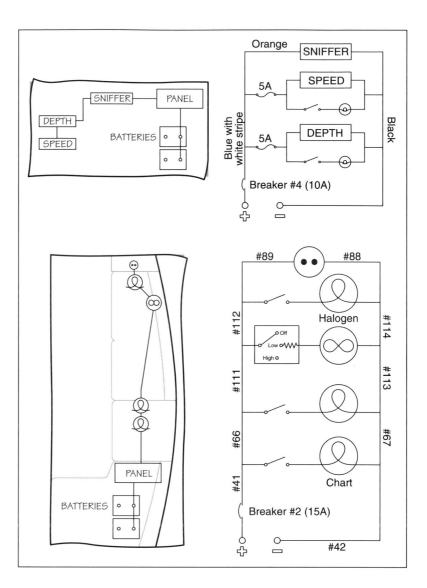

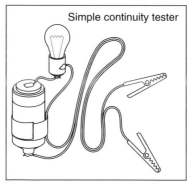

Simple continuity tester

For accurate circuit diagrams you will have to trace every wire. Wiring that disappears behind interior liners can be traced with a meter or a simple continuity tester. Be sure one end of the wire run is disconnected when checking for continuity.

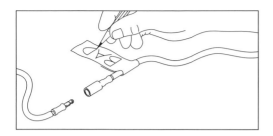

While you are tracing, pay attention to the condition of the wires and especially the connections. Tighten any that are loose and flag any that show signs of corrosion, also noting the problem on your drawing. You will come back later and take corrective measures.

MASTER DIAGRAM

The individual circuit drawings are perfectly adequate, but a master drawing will be more convenient. If you have access to a computer, a simple drawing program makes neat, legible wiring diagrams a snap, and it allows for later additions and corrections. A nearby copy center will print the diagram on a chart-size sheet of paper for a modest fee.

(If you are a Luddite, the back side of an old chart is ideal for accomplishing the same thing with pen and straightedge.)

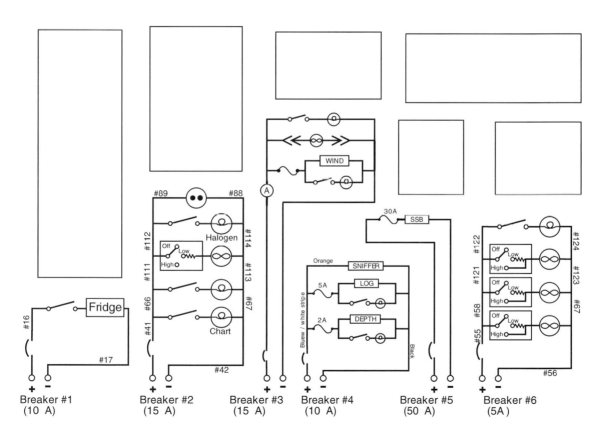

LAYOUT SCHEMATIC

An alternative to the simple circuit diagram is a layout schematic—essentially a combination of the component layout and the master wiring diagram. This has the advantage of showing not just the electrical path but also approximately how every electrical component in the boat is physically connected. Again, this type of drawing is easier to do on the computer.

SIGNAL WIRES

Signal wires connect transducer to depth sounder, radio to antenna, GPS to autopilot. Treat signal wires separately from power wires, mapping them on a separate drawing.

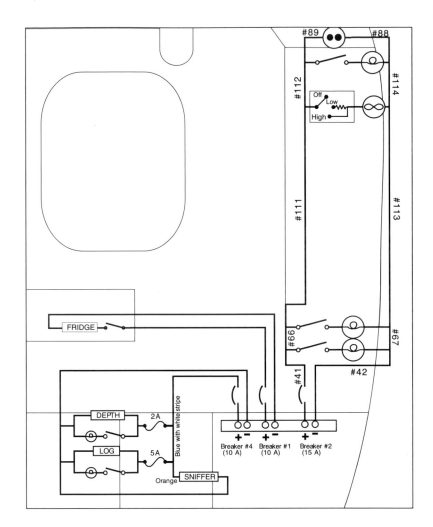

CHAPTER 6

TROUBLESHOOTING

" **I** s it plugged in?"

It is the obvious question and, along with changing a light bulb, usually exhausts the electrical troubleshooting repertoire of most of us. Fortunately nearly all troubleshooting of 12-volt circuits is essentially determining if everything is "plugged in."

When you are familiar with the components of a circuit, it is a very short step to being able to assess the health of that circuit. Since we have just worked our way through circuits, now is the time to take that step.

Toss away visions of oscilloscopes and pocket protectors. When you squeeze the trigger on the nozzle of your garden hose and no water comes out, you look back down the hose for a kink, check that the faucet is open. The process of determining why current fails to flow through a wire is just as logical and hardly more complicated.

Of course, it is even less complicated to dial up your electrician, but always selecting that option can cost you more than just money. Electrical problems don't occur only at the dock, and an electrician can be hard to come by at sea. You might muddle through a crippling electrical problem on your first try, but a bit of prior troubleshooting experience certainly improves the odds.

Spend a little time running tests on your boat's electrics. They might be revealing. At the very least you will be developing a skill that could turn out to be more valuable than you imagine.

SIGNS OF TROUBLE

Finding electrical problems sometimes requires just being observant.

HOUSE OF CARDS

IF DIM LIGHTS are caused by a corroded or loose connection, cleaning and tightening that connection may be all the corrective measures required. But if you determine that the problem is a low charge on the battery, simply recharging the battery may be inadequate. Why is the battery low? Maybe you just haven't run the engine. Maybe the battery is dying. Maybe the anchor light has been left on. Maybe a short is draining the battery. Maybe a leaking stuffing box is causing the bilge pump to run. Maybe the alternator belt is loose. Maybe the alternator is defective; maybe the regulator. The interconnected nature of a boat's electrical system makes it imperative to determine what *caused* a problem and to correct that condition as well.

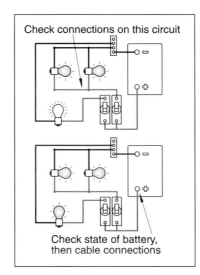

Check connections on this circuit

Check state of battery, then cable connections

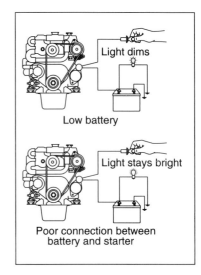

Light dims

Low battery

Light stays bright

Poor connection between battery and starter

DIMMING

Dim lights result from low voltage. Low voltage also slows fans and pumps and causes electronics to "crash." If only a single light or the lights on a single circuit are dim, the likely cause is a bad connection or inadequate wire size. When all lights are dim, suspect a low charge on the battery. Less likely is a poor connection between the battery and the distribution panel.

SLUGGISH STARTING

An anemic groan or just the click of the solenoid when you hit the starter button is the classic indicator of a "dead" battery, but a poor connection can exhibit the same symptoms. Observe an illuminated cabin lamp when the starter is engaged. Some dimming is normal, especially if the battery is a deep-cycle type, but if the lamp goes out, the battery is almost certainly low. If the lamp remains bright, look for a loose or corroded connection somewhere between the battery and the starter.

A defective starter motor is a less likely possibility.

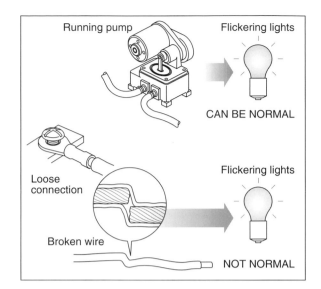

Running pump

Flickering lights

CAN BE NORMAL

Loose connection

Broken wire

Flickering lights

NOT NORMAL

FLICKERING

Flickering can be "normal" when it is caused by load variation—such as the cycling of a pump. Flickering that is not concurrent with the operation of some other appliance almost always indicates a loose or corroded connection or a broken wire.

BLOWN FUSE

When the lights go out you *know* you have an electrical problem. But a blown fuse is only a symptom. It means the circuit was overloaded. To avoid a recurrence, it is imperative to determine the cause of the overload and correct it.

If the overload is due to adding an appliance or upgrading to a component with higher wattage, substituting a larger fuse might be an acceptable solution, but only if all the wire in the circuit is capable of carrying the higher current. The inevitability of upgrading is reason enough to install wiring a size larger than immediate requirements.

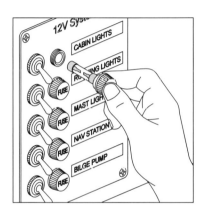

GROUND RETURN

THE ELECTRICAL ITEMS ON A MARINE ENGINE almost always use a ground-return circuit. That means the engine, rather than an insulated wire back to the battery, serves as the ground side of the circuit. Because components are electrically connected to the ground circuit by their mounting bolts, you must consider these mounts when you suspect a poor connection. A buildup of rust between mating surfaces can open the circuit as effectively as a disconnected battery cable. And speaking of battery cables, the ground-return circuit is typically completed through a cable connecting the engine block to the negative battery terminal. Be sure to check the connection of this cable to the engine.

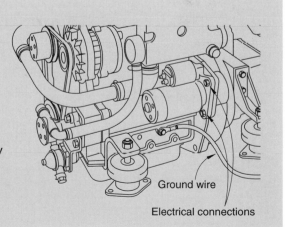

Ground wire

Electrical connections

HEAT

Wire too small for its load generates heat. If the wire gets hot enough, it can start a fire. Melted insulation is an all-too-common sign of less-disastrous wire heating. Treat such a discovery like chest pains—a fortunate warning you may not get again.

Wire the right size should not even get warm. As a matter of fact, heating usually occurs at junctions where a poor connection introduces resistance. It is a good idea to get in the habit of touching wires and connectors (12-volt only, PLEASE). If they are warm to the touch, they need attention. Aside from the danger (the problem will only get worse), resistance in the wiring means full voltage is not reaching the appliances in the circuit.

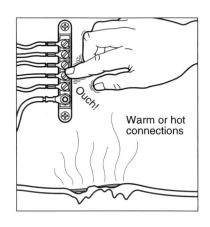

Warm or hot
connections

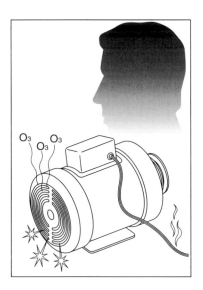

ODOR

The smell of hot insulation should lead you into a full-court press to find the source. Whether the insulation is burning due to a hot wire or contact with a hot engine, for example, is immaterial. Both circumstances place your boat at risk.

Another odor that should get your attention is ozone—that electric razor smell caused by electrical arcing. It is not uncommon for motors and generators to arc at their brushes, but equipment intended for marine use should be ignition protected—meaning either it should not produce sparks, or the arcing must be hermetically contained so it cannot be an ignition source. In the presence of propane that has leaked into the bilge, a spark is the equivalent of lighting a match. If you smell ozone, find the source and repair or replace the offending gear.

HEAT LOSS

IN CHAPTER 4 WE SAW that 100 feet (30 m) of 16-gauge wire has a resistance of 0.41 ohms, and if we push 10 amps through that resistance, we get a voltage drop of 4.1 volts (10A x 0.41Ω). What happened to that voltage? It was converted from electrical energy to heat energy. We can express this conversion in terms of power by multiplying the voltage drop times the current (P = V x I). In this case, we have 41 watts (4.1V x 10A) of power given up to heat. Spread over 100 feet of wire, this heat dissipates harmlessly, but what if the resistance is not due to small wire but rather a poor connection? Now we have 41 watts of power concentrated at a single point. The connection tries to become a light-bulb filament, until something melts.

If you are interested, you can reduce the two steps for calculating power loss to one: P = V x I, but since V = I x R, P = I x I x R or I^2R. Power lost as heat is often called I^2R loss.

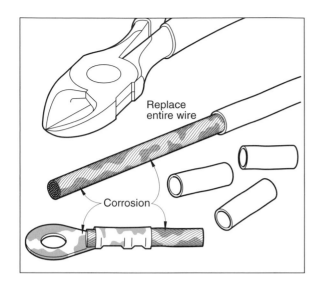

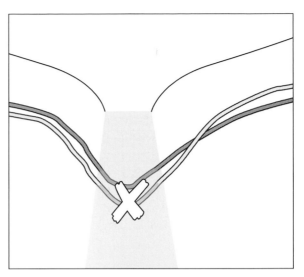

CORROSION

Electrical connections should be clean and bright. Clean away corrosion with a wire brush or bronze wool and coat the reassembled connection with petroleum jelly. Corrosion between wire and terminal requires cutting off the terminal and attaching a new one, but in this case you will often find that the wire inside the insulation is also corroded. If you cannot expose bright, unblemished wire, replace it.

WET WIRING

Any wire that is wet to the touch should be rerouted. Water and electrical wiring are a poor combination. Do not let wires lie in water or subject them to drips or drenchings.

RAT'S NEST

Wiring that is a tangled jumble is a bad sign. If previous "electricians" had no appreciation for the importance of neat and orderly wire runs, suspect that they also cut corners with regard to the type of wire and terminals used. A sloppy end product always suggests slipshod workmanship.

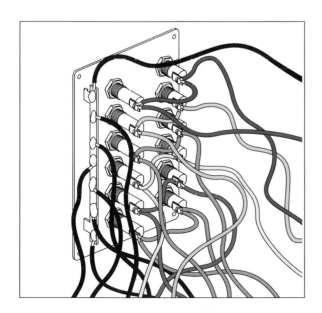

TEST LIGHT

You can diagnose a surprising number of common electrical problems by checking the circuit with a simple test light. This is essentially the same as checking a suspect outlet at home by plugging a lamp into it. If the lamp works, the outlet is fine.

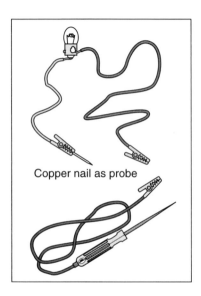

Copper nail as probe

MAKE OR BUY

A test light is easy enough to make by soldering leads to a 12-volt automotive bulb. Alligator clips on the leads let you clip one while you probe with the other—a nail in the gator's mouth makes a perfectly good test probe. But if you can't salvage the clips and bulb from your junk box, it will probably be cheaper to buy a ready-made tester. Appropriate 12-volt test lights—usually in the form of a probe with a light in the handle and a single clip-fitted wire lead—can be purchased for a couple of dollars at automotive supply stores.

USING A TEST LIGHT

ISOLATE THE FAULT

Connect one side of your test light to the negative side of the power source—in this case the battery—and methodically check the circuit by touching the probe to every junction. When the lamp fails to light, you have found the component or section of the circuit that is faulty. In this example, we find no power on the output side of the switch even though it is in the on position. The switch (or its connection) is faulty.

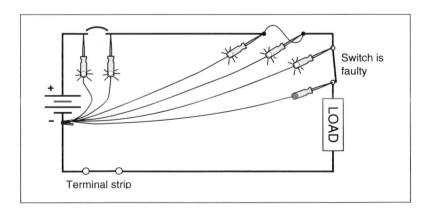

Switch is faulty

LOAD

Terminal strip

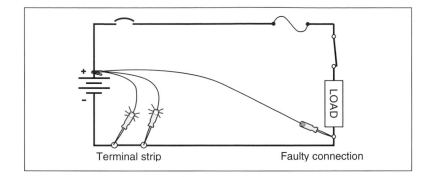

Terminal strip   Faulty connection

CHECK THE RETURN SIDE

What if you clipped the tester to the negative battery terminal and found voltage with every probe, all the way to the nonfunctioning appliance? Move the clip to the positive battery terminal and test the return side of the circuit.

FIND AN OPEN CIRCUIT

Because the bulb filament has higher resistance than hook-up wire, we wouldn't expect the test lamp to light if connected in parallel to one leg of a circuit. But if the circuit is open between the test probes, the lamp is now in series and should glow. Note that it may be dim because it is sharing the available voltage with other components in the circuit. If the tester lights when connected around a fuse holder, the fuse is bad. Connected around a switch, the tester should come on when the switch is in the off position, and it should go off when the switch is turned on.

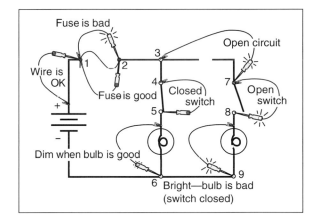

NARROW THE POSSIBILITIES

We have tested much more of this circuit than we needed to. If the 20-watt light works, it is a hard-wired test light, confirming power at junctions 3 and 6. We can clip our test light to junction 3 and test only the branch of the circuit supplying the 9-watt light. If neither light works, we should look for the problem on the battery side of junctions 3 and 6.

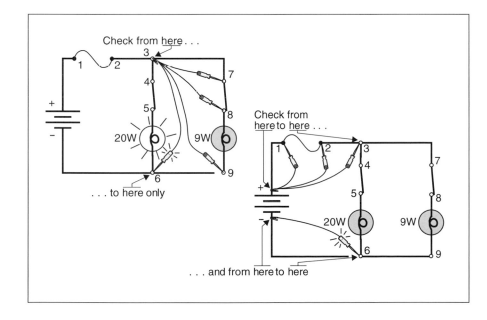

DIGITAL MULTIMETER

On today's sailboats, a multimeter is as essential as a rigging knife or an oil-filter wrench. Once you exceed the limited capabilities of a test light, you simply cannot troubleshoot electrical circuits effectively without a meter. A basic meter capable of measuring volts, ohms, and milliamps can be purchased for under $25 and is adequate for most tests you are likely to perform. If your budget allows it, a meter that allows direct current measurements up to 10 amps may eventually prove more versatile.

DIGITAL VS. ANALOG

Analog meters—meters with a needle—have served previous generations well, but like computers versus typewriters, modern digital meters are far superior. They are notably more accurate and much easier to use, especially for the novice. In addition, analog meters often alter the tested circuit—called meter loading—because they add a parallel circuit. This results in erroneous readings. Digital meters are connected the same way, but extremely high internal resistance makes the connection virtually invisible to the circuit. If you have an analog meter, donate it to a school and buy yourself a digital meter.

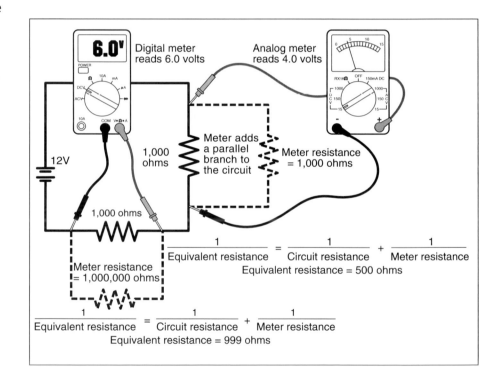

Digital meter reads 6.0 volts

Analog meter reads 4.0 volts

Meter adds a parallel branch to the circuit

Meter resistance = 1,000 ohms

12V

1,000 ohms

1,000 ohms

$$\frac{1}{\text{Equivalent resistance}} = \frac{1}{\text{Circuit resistance}} + \frac{1}{\text{Meter resistance}}$$

Equivalent resistance = 500 ohms

Meter resistance = 1,000,000 ohms

$$\frac{1}{\text{Equivalent resistance}} = \frac{1}{\text{Circuit resistance}} + \frac{1}{\text{Meter resistance}}$$

Equivalent resistance = 999 ohms

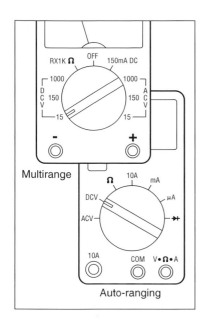

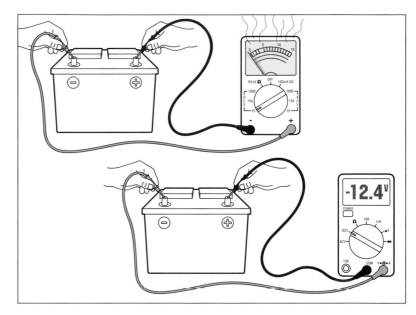

AUTO RANGING

Since you don't always know what reading to expect, standard practice has always been to select the highest range setting, then "tap" the probes to make sure the reading isn't still going to "peg" the meter. If not, you switch down in range until reach the one appropriate for the reading. With an auto-ranging meter, you simply select what you want to measure—volts, amps, or ohms—and the meter does the rest. This is not only convenient, it greatly reduces the likelihood of meter damage. If you are buying a meter, get one that auto ranges.

POLARITY

Another reason for tapping probes is to make sure the needle deflects in the right direction. If not, polarity is reversed and you need to reverse the probes. Nearly all digital meters have automatic polarity, measuring voltage or current with the probes connected either way. Polarity is typically indicated on these meters with a + or − in the display.

CLAMP-ON METERS

A multimeter that measures currents up to about 10 amps—the usual limit—more than satisfies the requirements of most boatowners, but if you want to measure starting currents, charging currents, or current flows to high-demand devices like inverters and windlasses, you need a clamp-on meter. Through magic known as Hall effect, this type of meter measures the current flowing through any wire passing through the center of the clamp. Clamp-on meters measure currents of 1,000 amps or more with the not insignificant advantage that they don't have to be connected into the circuit. They are less accurate for low currents.

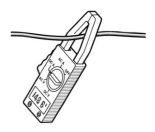

METER FUNDAMENTALS

Your particular meter should have a user's manual, but here are the basics of connecting a multimeter to the circuit.

CONNECTING TEST LEADS

If the test leads are removable, the black lead is always plugged into the jack labeled COM—*common* to all tests. For voltage and resistance tests, the red lead goes into the jack labeled V/Ω. For current measurements, plug the red lead into the jack marked A or 10A. Some meters have a separate jack labeled mA for measuring smaller currents.

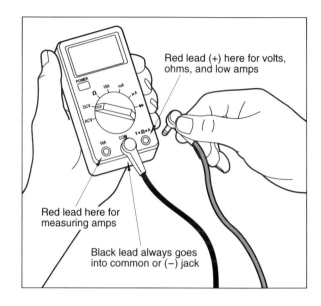

Red lead (+) here for volts, ohms, and low amps

Red lead here for measuring amps

Black lead always goes into common or (–) jack

MEASURING VOLTAGE

The voltmeter functions like the test light except that it tells you exactly how much voltage is present. Set the selector switch to V or DC V and touch the leads to any two points in the circuit. If there is a difference in potential between the two points, the meter will display it in volts.

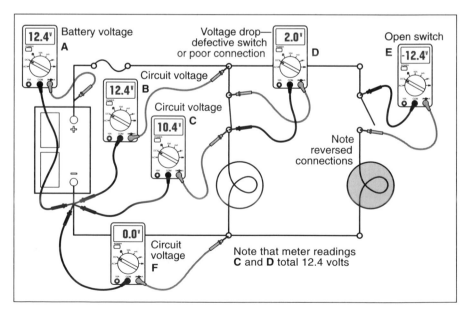

Battery voltage **A** — 12.4ᵛ

Voltage drop— defective switch or poor connection **D** — 2.0ᵛ

Open switch **E** — 12.4ᵛ

Circuit voltage **B** — 12.4ᵛ

Circuit voltage **C** — 10.4ᵛ

Note reversed connections

Circuit voltage **F** — 0.0ᵛ

Note that meter readings **C** and **D** total 12.4 volts

MEASURING CURRENT

The ammeter must be connected in series with a conductor to measure current flow. That means you have to break the circuit and insert the ammeter at the break. Check the size of the breaker or fuse in the circuit to make certain expected amperage does not exceed the capacity of your meter.

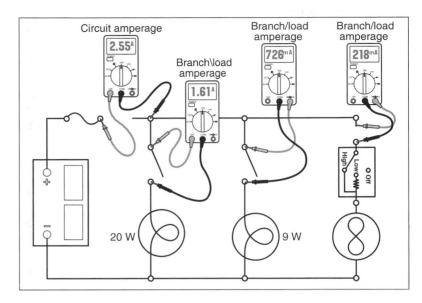

Even when the breaker is a 15-amp unit, you can often test the circuit with a 10-amp meter provided you operate only one appliance on the circuit at a time. Do not use a 10-amp meter to test starter motor or windlass circuits, or any other load that might exceed 10 amps.

MEASURING RESISTANCE (OR LACK THEREOF)

The ohmmeter measures resistance, and the component you are testing *must be disconnected from the circuit.* Otherwise, the meter is also measuring the resistance around the rest of the circuit. The meter can also be damaged if there is power in the circuit. When making resistance measurements, always turn off the circuit.

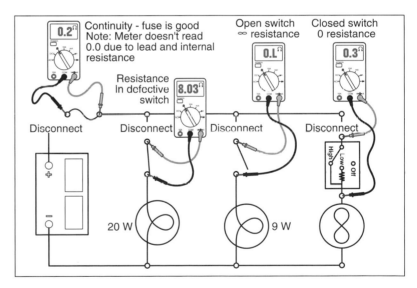

The safest practice is to confirm that the circuit is open with your voltmeter before doing resistance tests. If the circuit branches, disconnect one end of the component you are testing to isolate it.

Often you will use the ohmmeter to test for continuity rather than resistance. An unrestricted conductor will read near zero on the ohmmeter. An open circuit reads ∞ or O.L (overload).

The boatowner adept with a multimeter can quickly identify and pinpoint almost any electrical problem likely to occur on a boat. The following provides visual guidance.

Caution: Always double-check meter setting and test-lead connections before you attempt any tests. Modern meters are better protected against operator error, but you will still blow the meter's internal fuse if, for example, you intend to check battery voltage but have the meter set to check current. Verify the setting.

VOLTMETER TESTS

BATTERY VOLTAGE

With all circuits off *and the battery rested*, touching the probes to the battery terminals yields battery voltage. If you are using a digital voltmeter, this test can provide a fair assessment of the state of charge—if you know the fully charged rest voltage of the tested battery. The rule of thumb is that every 0.01 volts below the fully charged voltage equals a 1.25% discharge.

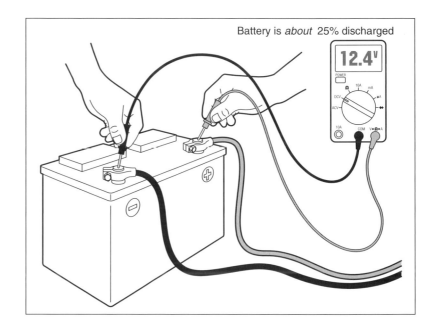

Battery is *about* 25% discharged

MULTIMETER CONNECTIONS

Voltmeter—Parallel

Ammeter—Series

Ohmmeter—Isolated

ZERO ADJUST

ANALOG METERS have an *Ohms Adjust* knob that allows you to set the meter to zero resistance when the probes are crossed. Digital meters rarely incorporate this adjustment, so always cross the probes of a digital meter first before taking a resistance measurement to determine the internal resistance caused by the leads and fuse. It is normally tiny, on the order of 0.4 ohms, but it will prevent a zero ohms reading even on a perfect conductor.

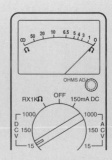

CHECKING YOUR HYDROMETER

IN CHAPTER 3, I pointed out that cell voltage is equal to the specific gravity plus 0.84. Check this for yourself by measuring the specific gravity for each cell, converting each reading to volts (V = SG + 0.84), adding the cell voltages together, and comparing them to your meter reading. Some disparity can be expected due to minor inaccuracies in hydrometer readings, but if the two voltages disagree by as much as 0.10 volts, try a different hydrometer. Poor calibration is common.

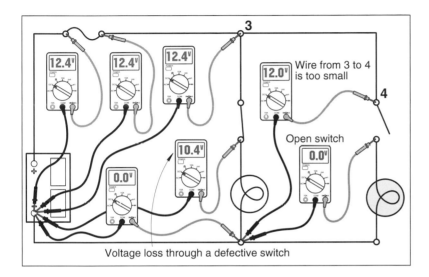

Voltage loss through a defective switch

CIRCUIT VOLTAGE

With the black probe attached to the negative battery post, you can verify the voltage at every junction in the circuit. Remember that we don't want the total voltage drop between battery and appliance to exceed 3 percent. If battery voltage is 12.4 volts and we read 12 volts at the appliance, there is excessive resistance in the circuit.

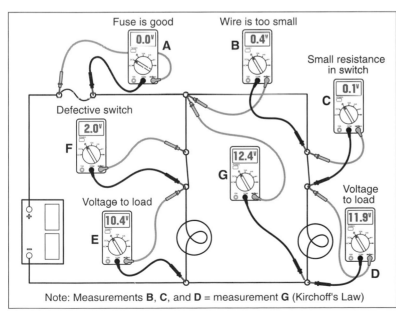

Note: Measurements **B**, **C**, and **D** = measurement **G** (Kirchoff's Law)

VOLTAGE DROP

Rather than calculate voltage drop across some section or component of the circuit, we can measure it directly by bridging it with the multimeter. Remember that voltage drop is directly proportional to current (V = I x R), so measure it with the circuit under maximum load.

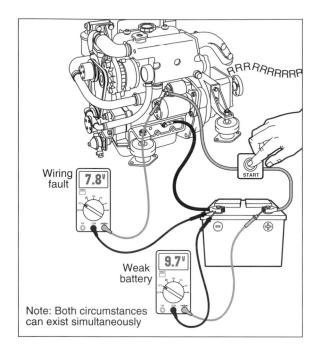

Wiring fault **7.8ᵛ**

Weak battery **9.7ᵛ**

Note: Both circumstances can exist simultaneously

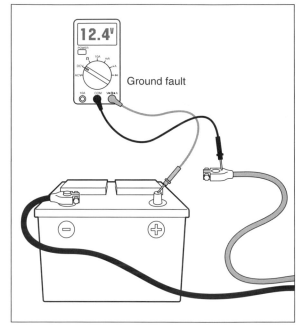

12.4ᵛ

Ground fault

LOAD VOLTAGE

Heavy starter current commonly pulls battery voltage down, but if voltage measured at the battery posts when the starter is engaged declines below 10 volts, need for a bigger battery is indicated. If voltage at the battery remains high, but falls at the load, the trouble is in the wiring.

A 0.1-ohm resistance will show up as a 0.2-volt drop if the circuit has a 2-amp load ($V = I \times R$)—seemingly not a problem in a cabin-light circuit. But if this small resistance is between the battery post and cable clamp, and we hit the starter button, drawing 150 amps, the voltage drop leaps to 15 volts—effectively an open circuit since we have only 12 volts available.

GROUND FAULT

Any current flowing to "earth" discharges batteries and may result in destructive corrosion. Such short circuits—called ground faults—are easy to detect. With all circuits off, a voltmeter connected between the positive battery post and the disconnected cable reads zero if no electrical path exists to ground. A voltage reading indicates a ground fault. Leaks are most often caused by moisture, faulty insulation, poor wiring, or defective switches. Trace the leak with the ammeter setting (see below).

EXTENDING YOUR REACH

TO MAKE VOLTMETER USE more convenient, make up a test-lead extension—a 20-foot (6 m) length of flexible (type 3) #16 wire with alligator clips on both ends. Clip one end to the "ground" point for the circuit—usually the negative battery post or the negative bus bar in the distribution panel—and clip the other end to the meter's common (black) probe. If you are measuring circuit voltage, be sure your reference voltage is with the extension in use.

KIRCHOFF'S LAW

NOTE THAT WHEN we check the battery voltage of an energized circuit, we are also measuring the voltage drop through the entire circuit. The total of the voltage drops in a circuit is always equal to the source voltage. This is called *Kirchoff's Law*, and it explains the detriment of voltage drops. If a defective switch uses 2 volts, we only have 10.4 volts left to supply a load designed to operate on 12 volts. Turning this around, if you measure a 10.4-volt drop across the load but 12.4 volts at the battery, somewhere in the circuit you will find additional voltage drops totaling 2 volts. It is just sums, and it tells you a lot about what you are looking for when you troubleshoot a circuit.

OHMMETER TESTS

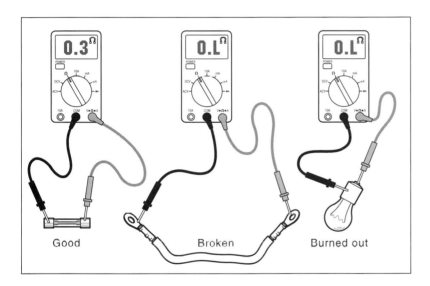

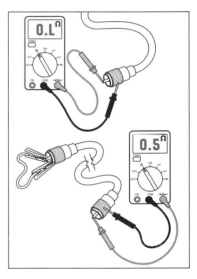

CHECKING CONDUCTANCE

Touching the probes to the ends of an isolated conductor shows you its resistance. A good wire or fuse will have little or no measurable resistance. An O.L (overload) or ∞ reading indicates a broken wire, blown fuse, or some other type of open circuit.

TESTING COAX

Disconnect the coax at both ends and touch the meter probes to the center pin and the body of one of the connectors. O.L is the only allowable meter reading. Clip a jumper wire between the pin and the body of this connector, then do the same test at the opposite end. Now the meter should read near zero, confirming unbroken conductors and uncorroded plug connections.

MASTHEAD LIGHTS

TEST THE NORMAL RESISTANCE of masthead light circuits by disconnecting (or unplugging) the wires at the deck and measuring the resistance of the circuit. Record the meter reading. When the light later fails, you can determine from the deck if the problem is an open circuit, probably a burned-out bulb (meter reads O.L), a corroded connection (meter reads more than normal but less than O.L), a short in the wiring (meter reads near zero), or a short to the mast (meter reads less than O.L when one probe is across both wires and the other touches the mast). In this last instance, be sure your fingers aren't touching the metal portion of the probes, or the "short circuit" resistance you will be measuring will actually be your body resistance.

If the meter reads O.L, twist the wires together before you go to the top of the mast. At the top, remove the bulb and check it with your meter; O.L means the bulb is burned out. Also test the resistance across the socket; with the wires twisted together at the bottom the reading should be near the wire resistance. For example, the resistance of #12 wire is about 0.16 ohms per 100 feet (30 m) (see Chapter 4), so on a 40-foot (12 m) stick wired with #12 wire, the ohmmeter reading should be near 0.13 ohms (0.8 x 0.16). With a crossed-probe resistance of 0.4 ohms, the meter reading for good wires should be around 0.5 ohms. Higher resistance suggests corrosion. O.L indicates a broken wire or a faulty connection.

Small wire or corroded connections

0.9

Short to mast

1.2

Open circuit

0.L

Short circuit

0.7

Normal

8.4

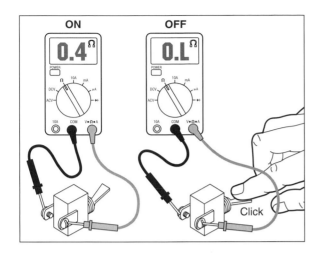

TESTING SWITCHES

With the probes in contact with the switch terminals, the ohmmeter should read O.L with the switch off, zero when you turn the switch on. All other readings suggest replacement.

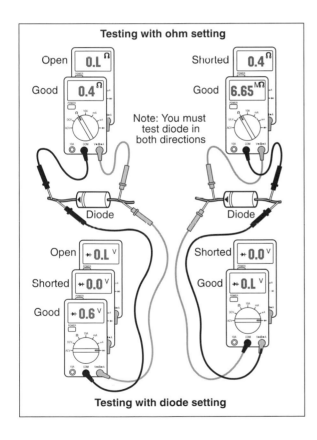

DIODE TESTING

Diodes are electrical check-valves, passing current in one direction but resisting the flow in the opposite direction. A functioning diode will register low resistance when tested in one direction, high resistance when the probes are reversed. If the meter reads near the same in both directions—whether high or low—the diode is defective.

FINDING SHORT CIRCUITS

A blown fuse or burned wire indicates an overload, often caused by a "short" in the circuit that lets current bypass the load. Note that damage from a short often occurs away from the fault, in the most resistive part of the circuit.

First remove the load component and test it. A near-zero reading across the terminals of an appliance usually indicates an internal short. If the appliance is good, the short is in the circuit.

Shorts are easier to diagnose when the expected resistance is O.L, so leave the load out of the circuit and connect the meter in its place. Be sure the battery is also disconnected. The meter should read O.L; any other reading indicates a short. Opening and reclosing the circuit methodically will pinpoint the location of the short. When a break in the circuit has no effect on the meter reading, the short is on the meter side of the opening; if the meter reading jumps to O.L, the short is on the other side.

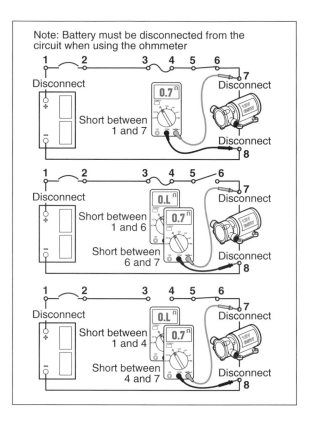

Note: Battery must be disconnected from the circuit when using the ohmmeter

EVALUATING A GROUND FAULT

If you found a ground fault when you connected the voltmeter between the positive battery post and its disconnected cable, you can determine how serious that leak is by connecting the ohmmeter between the disconnected positive *cable* and the *negative* battery post. This measures the resistance of the ground fault.

If the meter reads less than 10 ohms, your "leak" is probably a piece of gear you failed to turn off for this test. Otherwise, the lower the reading, the more serious the leak. But even though battery drain may be negligible with a high resistance fault ($I = V / R$), even a tiny current leaking to ground through some metal component of the boat can cause destructive corrosion. Use your ammeter to locate (as described below) any ground fault less than 10,000 ohms.

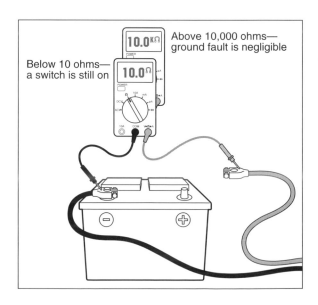

Above 10,000 ohms— ground fault is negligible

Below 10 ohms— a switch is still on

CHANGING RESISTANCE

YOU CAN USE OHM'S LAW to calculate the ohmmeter reading you might expect when you touch the meter probes to the terminals or contacts of an appliance. However, Ohm's Law calculates operating resistance; "cold" resistance can be much lower. Incandescent bulbs in particular show a fraction of calculated resistance when they are not illuminated. Likewise, electric motors may give a lower reading than expected. Before assuming an internal short, compare your reading to one taken on a similar appliance that you know is good.

ESTIMATING CIRCUIT CURRENT

With the circuit disconnected from power, connect the ohmmeter to the battery ends of the circuit to measure its total resistance. Be sure all breakers and switches are on. Divide the meter reading into battery voltage (12.6 V) to determine the expected current in the circuit—and whether you can safely use your ammeter in this circuit.

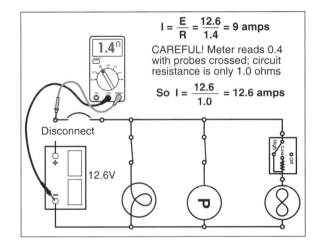

$$I = \frac{E}{R} = \frac{12.6}{1.4} = 9 \text{ amps}$$

CAREFUL! Meter reads 0.4 with probes crossed; circuit resistance is only 1.0 ohms

$$\text{So } I = \frac{12.6}{1.0} = 12.6 \text{ amps}$$

AMMETER TESTS

POWER CONSUMPTION

Manufacturers are sometimes "optimistic" in rating the current requirements of their equipment. By inserting an ammeter in the circuit, you can measure the actual current draw. It is a good exercise to update your load-calculation chart (Chapter 3) with actual measurements.

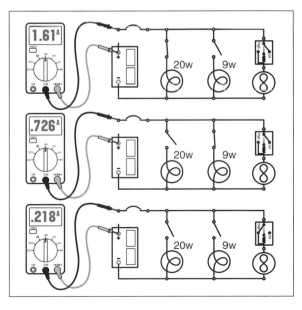

TRACING GROUND FAULTS

The sensitivity of an ammeter makes it ideal for tracing the tiny currents that often leak, sometimes with dire consequences, from boat wiring. With all breakers off, connect the meter between the positive battery post and the disconnected positive cable. One at a time, disconnect any circuits connected directly to the cable clamp or otherwise unfused. If the leak disappears, it is on the just-disconnected circuit. If the leak persists, check each breaker with your ohmmeter. It should read O.L when the breaker is open.

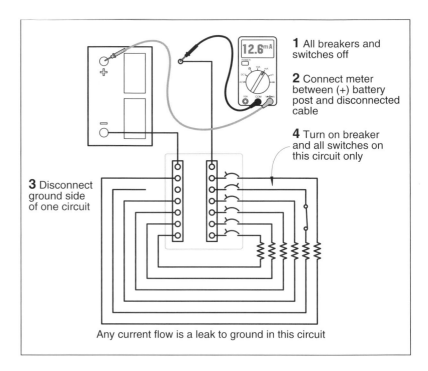

1 All breakers and switches off

2 Connect meter between (+) battery post and disconnected cable

4 Turn on breaker and all switches on this circuit only

3 Disconnect ground side of one circuit

Any current flow is a leak to ground in this circuit

Testing the wiring beyond the breakers—which is most of the boat's wiring—requires disconnecting the ground side of each individual circuit one at a time. With the ammeter between the positive post and the disconnected cable, and with all other breakers off, turn on the breaker and all switches in the ungrounded circuit. If any current flows, it is leaking from this circuit into one of the ones still connected to ground. If the leak is to a metal through-hull fitting—a common occurrence—and finding its way back to ground outside the boat, it is doing more than draining your battery. This is called stray current, and It is destroying the involved through-hull. It is essential to track down and eliminate any stray currents that exceed 5 milliamps.

CHAPTER 7

CHARGING SYSTEMS

As soon as your boat is beyond the reach of an extension cord, the only way to replace power you drain from your batteries is by generating it. For more than half a century that has meant a belt-driven generator/alternator combined with a mechanical/electronic regulator, both borrowed virtually unchanged from the automobile industry. Only in the last decade have we begun to see charging equipment designed specifically for the unique requirements of sailboat electrical systems.

Because the primary propulsion of a sailboat is the wind (sadly, today this is a disputable proclamation), a sailboat's engine may not run enough performing its chief function for the engine-driven alternator to satisfy the vessel's electrical needs. The traditional solutions to this shortfall have been to motor rather than sail—contrary to the reasons for owning a sailboat—and/or resort to the equally distasteful practice of running the engine with the boat anchored. This latter option not only rends tranquility with the clatter of a reciprocating iron, In the long run it is damaging to the diesel engine.

A partial solution is the marine regulator, designed to charge batteries at their maximum acceptance level. Where battery capacity merits, this regulator can be combined with a more powerful alternator. One or both of these enhancements reduces charging times, sometimes dramatically.

For those wanting to pare engine time even more, perhaps eliminate it altogether, alternative energy sources are available that can partially or fully meet a sailboat's typical electrical requirements. Of these, solar power is perhaps the most attractive because solar panels have no moving parts. However, wind generators offer higher capacity from a smaller package. And even the smallest water-powered generator will usually satisfy all charging requirements of a boat on passage.

This chapter will show you how to configure an effective charging system, how to connect it, and how to keep it operating at peak efficiency.

ALTERNATORS

The engine-powered alternator remains the primary charging source on most sailboats.

OUTPUT

Alternators are often rated at about 6,000 rpm rotor speed, but most sailboat charging is done with the engine at idle speed, around 800 rpm. With a 2-to-1 pulley ratio (see sidebar), that translates into a rotor speed of 1,600 rpm. Most alternators will put out less than 30% of rated output at this speed. Heat also decreases output by as much as 25%. To determine the actual output of your existing alternator you will have to measure it (using a high-capacity ammeter, **NOT** your 10-amp multimeter) with the batteries deeply discharged so the regulator allows maximum output.

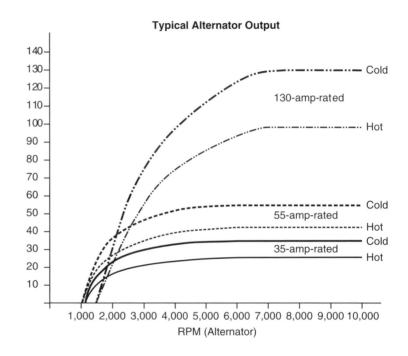

Typical Alternator Output

If you are buying an alternator, be sure you find out the hot rating (200°F or 93°C) for the rotor speed that corresponds to your charging pattern. As a general rule alternators should not run continuously at more than about 75% of their rated maximum.

PULLEY RATIO

WHERE THE ALTERNATOR PULLEY is $2\frac{1}{2}$ inches (6.4 cm) in diameter and the one on the engine is 5 inches (12.7 cm), the pulley ratio is 2 (5 ÷ 2.5). That means the alternator rotor makes 2 revolutions for each engine revolution. At 800 engine rpm, the alternator is turning 1,600 rpm.

It is relatively simple to fit the alternator with a smaller pulley or the engine with a larger one to increase rotor speed. The limiting factor is the maximum safe rpm for the alternator, usually 10,000 rpm. Dividing maximum rotor rpm by maximum engine rpm provides the largest safe pulley ratio. For an engine rated at 3,600 rpm, that ratio is 2.78 (10,000 ÷ 3,600).

Multiply the alternator pulley by this ratio or divide the drive pulley by it, depending on which you want to change. For example, 2.78 times $2\frac{1}{2}$ gives us an engine-pulley size of 6.95, so a 7-inch (18 cm) pulley will be the optimum size for getting the highest output at idle without overspinning the alternator at higher engine speeds. Rotor speed increases to 2,224 rpm at 800 engine rpm, which more than doubles alternator output.

Drive Pulley Selection				
Drive Pulley	Alternator Pulley	Ratio	Engine RPM	Alternator RPM
5-inch		2	1,000	2,000
			3,600	7,200
6-inch	$2\frac{1}{2}$-inch	2.4	1,000	2,400
			3,600	8,640
7-inch		2.8	1,000	2,800
			3,600	10,080
8-inch		3.2	1,000	3,200
			3,600	11,520

SIZING

Batteries should not be charged at a rate that much exceeds 25% of capacity. So if your boat's total battery capacity is, say, 200 Ah, an alternator capable of putting out about 50 amps provides all the charging capacity you can use.

To get 50 amps with the alternator hot and the engine at idle speed, you may have to buy an alternator rated at 70 or 80 amps. Beyond that, more charging capacity is wasted—unless you are running other electrical equipment while charging. In that case increase the alternator size by the current requirements of the equipment.

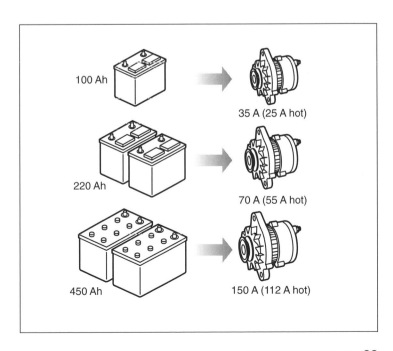

100 Ah → 35 A (25 A hot)

220 Ah → 70 A (55 A hot)

450 Ah → 150 A (112 A hot)

IGNITION PROTECTION

If you have a gasoline engine or LPG (propane) appliances, the alternator should be ignition protected. Automotive alternators are not ignition protected.

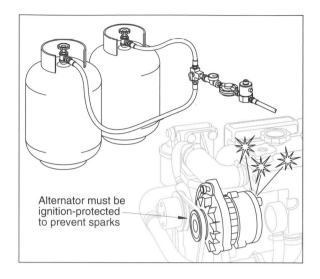

Alternator must be ignition-protected to prevent sparks

EXPECTING TOO MUCH

Because conventional batteries safely accept a 25% charge for only a short period of time, installing a larger alternator may reduce charging times less than you expect. Let's consider the replacement of a 50-amp alternator with one rated at 100 amps to charge a 400 Ah bank. If you discharge the batteries to 50% or more before charging, the big alternator will turn out maximum amperage for perhaps 10 minutes before the regulator starts cutting it back to a level compatible with declining battery acceptance. At the end of the first hour, the large alternator will have replaced perhaps 70 amp-hours. It takes the small alternator about 25 minutes longer to reach this charge level. For the remainder of the charge, the outputs from both alternators are essentially the same. The large alternator takes $3^1/_2$ hours to reach the 90% charge level, the small one gets there in 3 hours and 55 minutes. That is less than an 11% improvement in charging times from a 100% increase in alternator capacity. AGM and gel batteries have a different acceptance profile, so for these batteries the benefits of a big alternator may be somewhat better.

Whatever the potential benefit, it is less when the batteries are not deeply discharged—a common scenario when the engine runs daily for mechanical refrigeration. At the 30% discharge level, the big alternator provides full amperage for less than 5 minutes before the regulator starts limiting it. The standard alternator, at half the peak output, takes 10 minutes to reach the same cut-back point. After that the charging profile for both units will be identical. Net reduction in total charging time: just 5 minutes.

One benefit not to be overlooked, however, is that for a given battery capacity, a larger alternator will operate at a lower percentage of capacity, potentially extending the life of the alternator. Some large alternators also provide higher amperage at engine idle speeds, but in general, low output alternators have more windings (because the wire can be thinner), so they give better low-RPM performance. If most charging is done at anchor, this is a significant consideration.

REGULATORS

The rate of charge should be high when the batteries are low but less as they approach full charge. Adjusting alternator output to match need is the job of the regulator.

Back in Chapter 2, I told you that a generator consists of a spinning magnet that induces electron flow in surrounding wire coils. The magnet in a marine alternator is an electromagnet. When the alternator is spinning, it doesn't generate electricity unless this magnet is energized. The regulator simply controls the current to this magnet, allowing us to turn the alternator off without disconnecting the drive belt or stopping the engine. The current that energizes the magnet is called the *field current*.

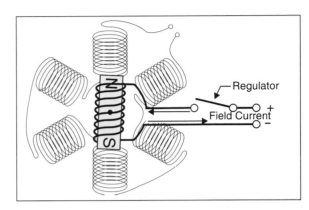

STANDARD REGULATOR

The basic regulator—manufactured by the millions for the automobile industry— is simple and trouble free. It is nothing more than an electronic switch that works like a spring-loaded magnetic switch. Closed, the switch provides current to the alternator's magnet, thus inducing alternator output. When voltage rises to a preset level, the switch opens, turning off the alternator. This causes output voltage to fall, but when it drops below the regulator's set voltage, the switch closes again. This all happens very rapidly—hundreds of times per second. The net effect is a rippling constant voltage and a pulsating current. As battery voltage rises, it takes less time for the alternator to elevate charging-circuit voltage to the cutout level, shortening "on" time. Voltage remains fixed, but shorter current pulses reduce the average current output.

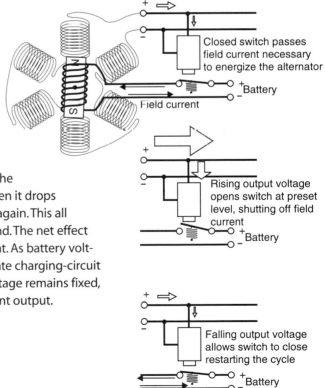

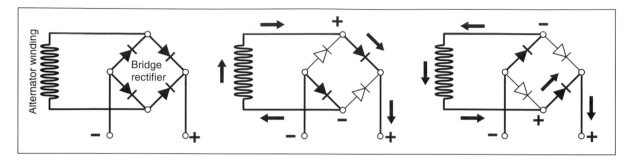

Of course, alternator output is AC and we need DC to feed our batteries. This is elegantly accomplished by passing the current through a diode array called a bridge rectifier. Acting like one-way gates, the diodes redirect half the current pulses, converting the output to pulsating DC. And that is all we need to know about rectification.

REGULATOR VOLTAGE

Generally, the higher the regulator voltage, the quicker the charge, but if charging voltage rises above around 14.4 volts, the batteries will begin to gas vigorously, lose electrolyte, and overheat. So the usual regulator choice for efficient charging is one that maintains output voltage at 14.4 volts (at 25°C/77°F).

However, once the battery nears full charge, 14.4 volts is too high, gassing the batteries vigorously and causing the positive plate to oxidize (corrode). If you continue to run the engine—perhaps motoring—a charging voltage of around 13.2 volts is ideal for maintaining full charge without overcharging. For years automobile manufacturers compromised on 13.8 volts—high enough to replace the shallow discharge from starting without later resulting in serious overcharging. And anyway, regulators are temperature compensated to lower output about 0.01 volts per degree centigrade of ambient temperature, so if the engine compartment warms by 50°C (90°F), a 13.8-volt regulator actually holds the alternator output at 13.3 volts.

Using a 13.8-volt regulator in a sailboat charging system nearly eliminates any risk of overcharging (the engine compartment heats up enough to derate the regulator), but charging times with a 13.8-volt regulator will be twice that of a 14.4-volt unit. Unless you motor a lot, expect your batteries to be chronically undercharged, leading to sulfation and early battery failure. Most sailboats should be fitted with the higher-voltage regulator. You will have to deal with the risk of overcharging in some other manner.

FIELD DISCONNECT

The simplest method of preventing a standard regulator from overcharging is with a switch in the field wire. When the battery is fully charged but you are continuing to run the engine, flipping the switch opens the field circuit, turning off the alternator. Where there is no ready access to the field wire, a switch in the excite circuit (see below) will do the same thing, but this requires stopping the engine, then restarting it.

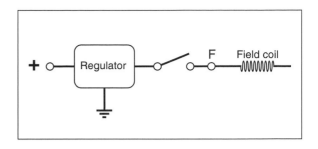

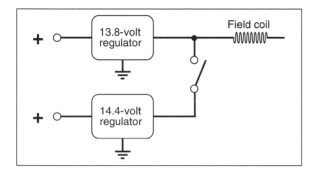

DUAL REGULATORS

Paralleling a 14.4-volt regulator with a 13.8-volt unit is only slightly more expensive—automotive regulators are dirt cheap—and this configuration lets the alternator continue to keep the battery in a fully charged state during long hours of motoring. When the switch is closed, the higher alternator output automatically shuts off the lower-voltage regulator. It is simple enough to put a timer switch in this circuit to make the voltage decrease semi-automatic.

FOOLING THE REGULATOR

As the engine room heats up, the output of a 14.4-volt regulator is likely to decline to around 13.9 volts—not ideal, but low enough not to hurt the batteries as long as you keep them supplied with water. But long engine hours are presumably the exception. It is more common for a sailor to want more output from the alternator, not less.

The voltage drop

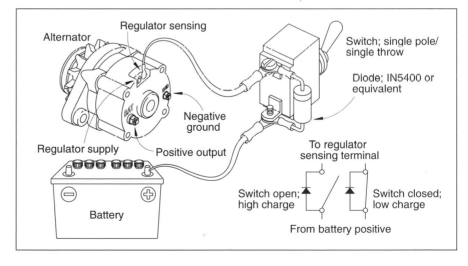

through a silicon diode is about 0.6 volt, so inserting a diode in the sensing wire fools the regulator into thinking battery voltage is lower than it really is. This causes the regulator to increase alternator output. Current in the sensing wire flows to the alternator, so be sure the cathode end of the diode—the marked end—is on the regulator/alternator side of the circuit.

This is a low-budget method of reducing charging time, and it requires some caution. Unless you know that your alternator is rated for continuous duty, be sure output doesn't rise above around 75% of its rated maximum for more than a few minutes. Monitor the batteries to make sure they do not get hot—above about 120°F. And you *must* remember to flip the switch to take the diode out of the circuit when the batteries start gassing vigorously. A timer minimizes the risk of costly forgetfulness.

MANUAL CONTROLLER

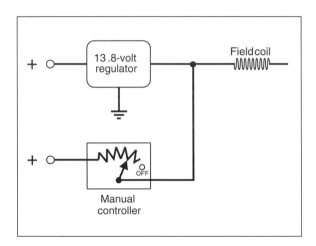

It is logical that the stronger the rotating magnet in an alternator, the more current flows, and vice versa. Since increasing the field current makes the electromagnet stronger, it also increases the alternator's output; reducing the field current reduces output. This provides another way to control alternator output. Rather than switching field current off and on, a manual controller adjusts the strength of the field current with a variable resistor—called a rheostat. This allows adjustment of alternator output exactly the same way you adjust light intensity with a dimmer switch. Unfortunately, forgetting that the current is cranked up, or even speeding up the engine without adjusting the controller (it is not actually "regulating" alternator output) can ruin the batteries, which happens with depressing regularity on boats fitted with manual controllers. Alternator control is best left to silicon instead of cerebrum.

THREE-STEP REGULATOR

A standard regulator is, in effect, a two-step regulator. It maximizes current output while letting the battery voltage rise to the set level, then it holds voltage constant and allows output current to decline. More sophisticated regulators charge the battery in three distinct phases.

BULK CHARGE
In the initial stage the alternator puts out maximum current until the battery voltage rises to around 14.4 volts. Assuming a 25% of battery amp-hour rating charge rate, the battery will be around 75% charged.

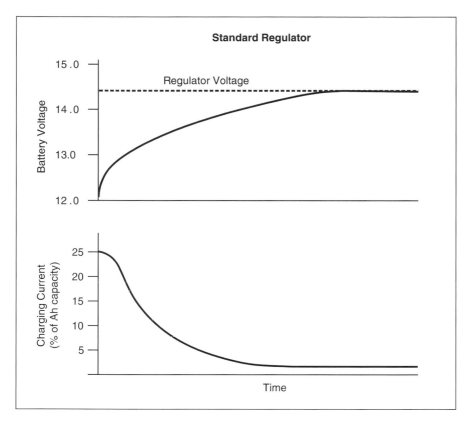

Standard Regulator

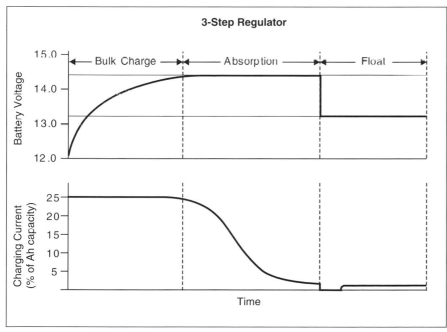

3-Step Regulator

ABSORPTION CHARGE

When voltage reaches 14.4, the regulator holds it there and allows the current to decline according to what the battery can accept. Ideally, this continues until charging current declines to 2% or 1% of the battery's amp-hour rating, indicating a charge level of around 90% or 95% respectively. In practice, most three-step regulators terminate the absorption phase based on time rather than current level.

FLOAT CHARGE

Triggered by time or current level, the regulator cuts voltage back to around 13.2 volts, which allows the engine to continue to run without overcharging the batteries.

EQUALIZATION—THE FOURTH STEP

Some "smart" regulators have a fourth phase intended to restore batteries to full capacity by converting inevitable sulfate deposits in the plates back into active material. This is accomplished by feeding a fixed current of less than 4% of amp-hour capacity to the battery until battery voltage rises to its maximum natural level—around 16.2 volts. This normally takes several hours. Equalization is only appropriate for heavy-duty deep-cycle batteries. Gel cells and AGM batteries are *never* equalized, and the high voltage is likely to do more harm than good to thinner-plate wet cells.

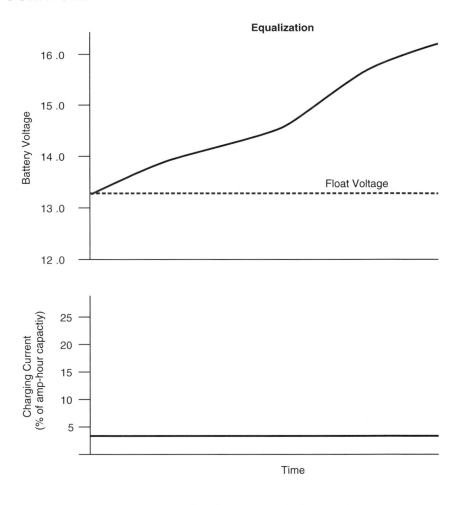

Equalize not more often than every 30 discharge cycles.

CHARGING GEL BATTERIES

WHILE SOME GEL BATTERIES purportedly can accept a bulk charge at current levels approaching 50% of battery amp-hour capacity, voltage cannot be allowed to exceed 14.1 volts. Taking advantage of a gel battery's high absorption requires a specialized regulator and usually a larger alternator.

ALTERNATOR AND REGULATOR WIRING

There are dozens, perhaps hundreds of different alternator and regulator combinations, so any help you find here is necessarily general in nature.

OUTPUT

The output terminal will be the largest terminal on the alternator and is nearly always labeled BAT, B+, or just +. You may find your alternator has two identical wires connected to the B+ terminal. Don't let this confuse you; for increased flexibility it is common to substitute parallel smaller wires for the large cable required for the high amperage of the alternator output.

ALTERNATOR TERMINAL DESIGNATIONS	
Output	B+, BAT, +
Negative	D−, E, GND, B−, −
Field	F, DF
Auxiliary	D+, 1, L, AUX, IND, 61
Tachometer	W, AC, R, STA, X, N, P
Sense	2, S

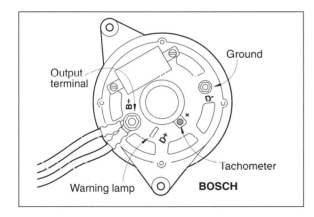

BOSCH

INTERNAL REGULATION

The regulator may be incorporated into the alternator. In this case the alternator may have only one or two other terminals. The one labeled D+, L, AUX, or sometimes 61 is the warning-lamp connection. If there is a tachometer feed, it is usually labeled R, W, or AC. A ground terminal, labeled GND, E (earth), B−, D−, or just − may also be provided. The S terminal on this Hitachi alternator is for the battery sensing wire.

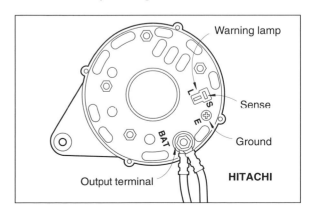

HITACHI

ATTACHED REGULATOR

Many alternators have a match-
ing regulator attached. Except
that the wiring and terminals are
typically located beneath the
regulator and accessible only by
removing the mounting screws,
attached regulators are connected to the alternator in the same
manner as an external regulator.

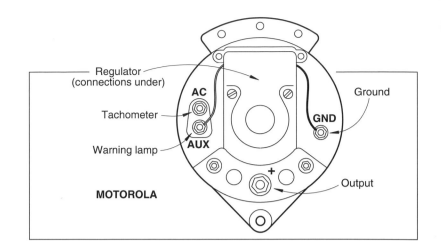

EXTERNAL REGULATION

Because they can be mounted
off the engine, external regulators have the advantage of running cooler, and they simplify servicing. An alternator configured
for an external regulator will
have a field terminal labeled F or
DF. The regulator's sensing wire is
usually connected to either the
D+ or the B+ terminal on the
alternator (machine sensed), or
to the positive terminal of the
house battery (battery sensed).

This connection also supplies
the power to most regulators.
The R terminal on the alternator

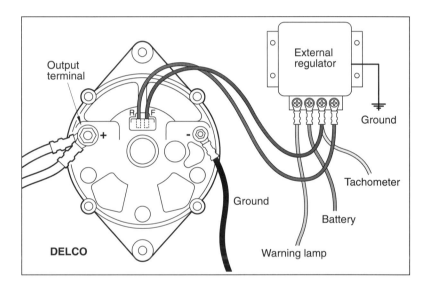

is unrectified output for the tachometer, and in this case it also disables the excite circuit when there is alternator output. Most external regulators also have a ground connection, which often is the housing.

POLARITY

Alternators generally fall into two types, P (positive) or N (negative), depending on which side of the field winding the regulator is located on. If the regulator is between the battery and the field winding, the alternator is a P-type. If the regulator is between the field winding and ground, it is an N-type alternator. Most externally regulated alternators are P-type; those with internal regulation are most often N-type.

With the batteries switched off and the field wire disconnected, you can determine type by checking the resistance between the F terminal and the ground. Near-zero resistance suggests a P-type; high resistance means the alternator is an N-type. (There are exceptions.) You only need to know this if you are changing regulators—to a three-step, for example—or if you need to "excite" the alternator.

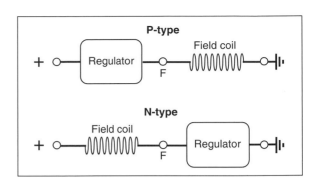

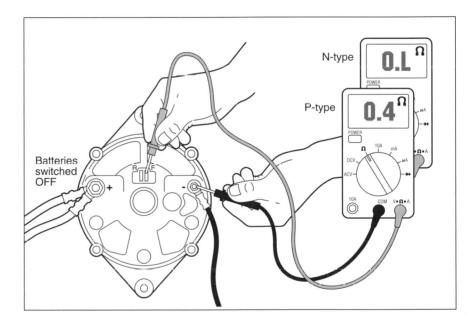

EXCITATION

Alternators don't operate until there is field current, but since most alternators supply their own field current, there isn't any until there is alternator output. This is something of a Catch-22. To overcome it, most alternators are "excited" with a temporary current

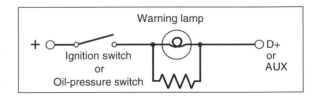

supplied by the battery, usually to the D+ terminal on the alternator. The engine-panel warning light is typically part of the excitation circuit. Once the alternator starts generating, the voltage on either side of the lamp is nearly the same, causing the lamp to go out. A resistor parallel to the lamp provides excitation current if the bulb burns out.

SURGE PROTECTION

The most common form of alternator failure is a direct result of opening the charge circuit while the alternator is running, usually due to mistakenly turning the battery-selector switch to OFF. This causes a high-voltage spike in the alternator windings that burns out some or all of the alternator's diodes. A surge protector such as Zap Stop (Heart Interface) shunts such a spike to ground and is especially recommended if the alternator is connected through a battery selector switch (see below).

Inadvertently reversing battery leads will also fry the diodes in your alternator.

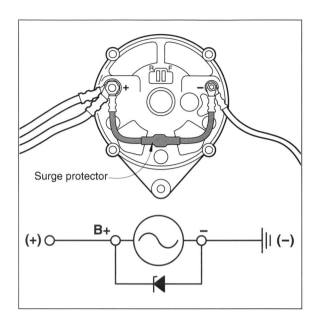

Surge protector

ALTERNATOR MAINTENANCE

BELTS

Make sure drive pulleys are aligned and drive belts are tight. Loosen (and retighten) both the pivot bolt and the tension-adjustment bolt. The best way to tighten a belt is with a tensioner fabricated from a turnbuckle; otherwise a dowel or wooden hammer handle to lever the alternator away from the engine will be less likely to cause damage than a metal tool. The rule of thumb is 10 pounds of pressure on the center of the belt's longest span should cause about $\frac{1}{2}$ inch deflection.

A $\frac{3}{8}$-inch belt is adequate for alternators up to around 70 amps. Up to about 130 amps, a single $\frac{1}{2}$-inch belt should handle the load, although dual belts are preferable. Beyond 130 amps, dual $\frac{1}{2}$-inch belts are essential to avoid belt slippage and/or excessive tension.

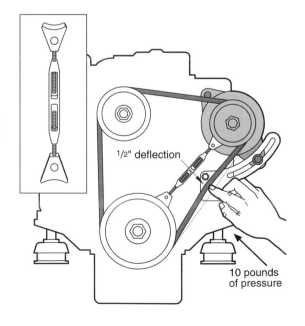

1/2" deflection

10 pounds of pressure

CONNECTIONS

High-frequency vibrations tend to loosen alternator connections and fatigue the wires. Check alternator wiring every 100 engine hours.

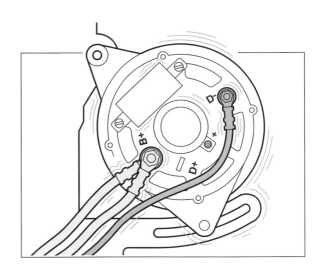

BEARINGS AND BRUSHES

You will avoid inopportune alternator failure if you have the bearings and brushes replaced every 3,000 engine hours.

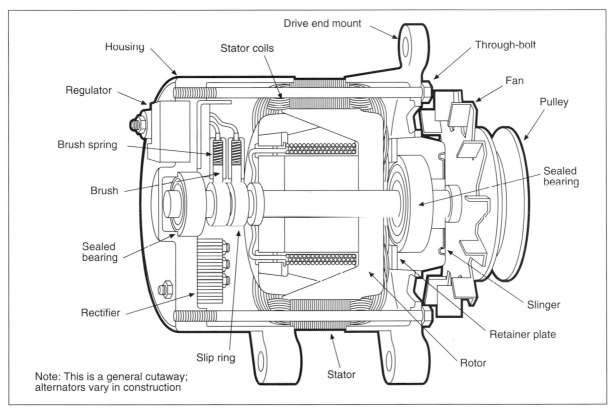

Note: This is a general cutaway; alternators vary in construction

TROUBLESHOOTING ALTERNATORS AND REGULATORS

Alternator repair is beyond the scope of this book, but a number of easy-to-correct problems can disable an otherwise healthy alternator. When regulation is external, it can be helpful to distinguish between regulator and alternator failure. In an emergency, it is possible to bypass the regulator. Remember: never disconnect the battery from a running alternator. Removing the load for even an instant will destroy the alternator's diodes.

ALTERNATOR OUTPUT

Measure terminal voltage at the battery, then start the engine. Voltage should increase by a volt or more. If not, check alternator output directly by touching volt-meter probes to the B+ terminal and the alternator case. CAUTION: WHEN TESTING ALTERNATOR OUTPUT, KEEP CLOTHES, HAIR, AND FINGERS CLEAR OF BELTS AND PULLEYS.

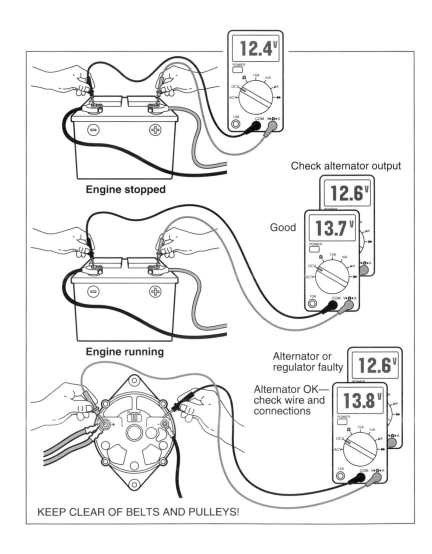

Engine stopped

Check alternator output

Good

Engine running

Alternator or regulator faulty

Alternator OK— check wire and connections

KEEP CLEAR OF BELTS AND PULLEYS!

With the battery near full charge—around 12.6 volts at rest—checking the alternator output at the B+ terminal after a few minutes of engine time will give you the output voltage set by the regulator. It will normally be 14.2 to 14.4 volts. Now check the voltage at the battery posts. Unless you run your engine a lot, anything less than 14 volts will result in chronic undercharging of your batteries. The problem is either resistance in the cables or a voltage drop caused by isolating diodes. (If you have a three-stage regulator, be sure it has not switched to float voltage.)

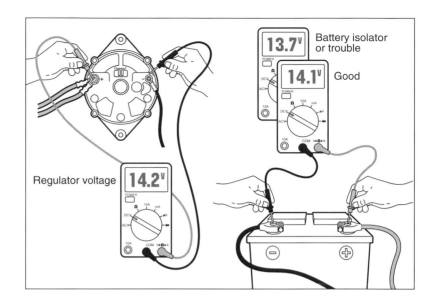

Battery isolator or trouble

Good

Regulator voltage

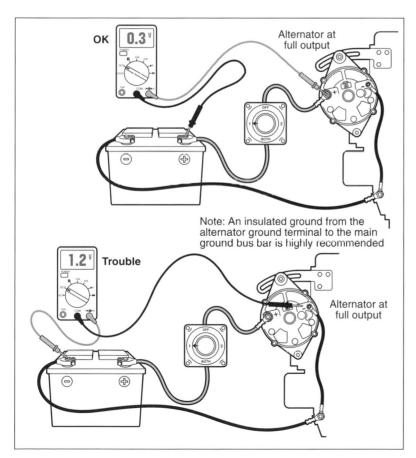

OK

Alternator at full output

Note: An insulated ground from the alternator ground terminal to the main ground bus bar is highly recommended

Trouble

Alternator at full output

Discharge the battery by turning on all lights for a few minutes. Start the engine and immediately—while the alternator is at full load—measure the voltage between the alternator's B+ terminal and the positive battery post. Voltage drop should be less than 0.5 volts, not more than 1 volt if you have a battery isolator in the circuit. Do the same test between the alternator case (ground) and the negative battery post. Excessive voltage drop indicates corrosion, poor connections, or undersized wire. Undersized wire is a common cause of chronic undercharging.

REGULATOR FAULTS

If voltage measured at the B+ terminal is *above* 14.4 volts, the regulator is faulty. A likely cause is a loose or broken sensing wire. Also make sure any diodes in the sensing circuit are oriented to allow current to flow *toward* the regulator.

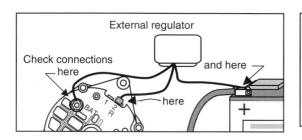

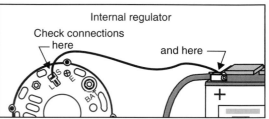

Battery voltage at B+ (or no voltage if you have isolating diodes in the charging circuit) means the alternator isn't charging, but the problem might still be the regulator. Check this with a test light fabricated from a 12-volt lamp of 10 to 15 watts. A common #93 automotive lamp is perfect.

Disconnect the regulator field wire from the F terminal on the alternator and protect it from shorting. Nearly all alternators with external regulators are P-type, so connect your lamp between the now-open F terminal and the positive post on the battery—or some other nearby source of battery power. (If the alternator output doesn't pass through external isolating diodes, you can use the B+ terminal.) This energizes the field circuit with the lamp limiting the current to around 1 amp. The lamp may or may not light. Start the engine. If you now measure the right voltage at B+, the likely problem is the regulator.

If the regulator is attached, removing it normally exposes the F terminal. If it isn't labeled, try your test light on all exposed terminals; you will not harm the alternator.

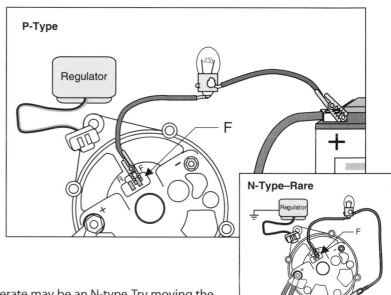

An alternator that still doesn't generate may be an N-type. Try moving the test lamp connection to ground and recheck B+ voltage. If the alternator generates, the regulator is defective.

If the test-light connection *to the battery* produced output, the alternator is a P-type and it generates. But before condemning the regulator, stop the engine and reconnect the field wire from the regulator. With the alternator running and one lead of the test lamp still connected to the positive post on the battery, touch the other momentarily to the F terminal. This is called *flashing the field*. If this starts the alternator and it keeps working, the problem is in the excitation circuit, and you can fix it.

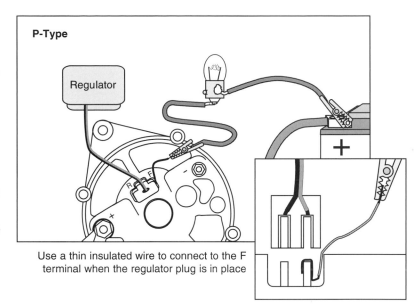

P-Type

Regulator

Use a thin insulated wire to connect to the F terminal when the regulator plug is in place

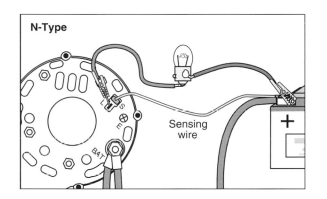

N-Type

Sensing wire

If none of the previous tests have produced output, reconnect the regulator wires and start the engine. With one side of the test lamp connected to the battery's positive post, touch the other side to the D+ terminal on the alternator. If the alternator is an N-type, this will flash the field and the alternator may start charging, indicating a problem with the excitation circuit.

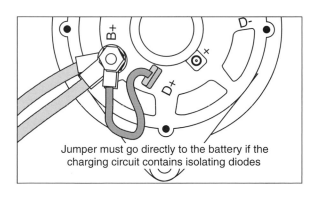

Jumper must go directly to the battery if the charging circuit contains isolating diodes

If the alternator starts charging when you touch the test lamp to the D+ terminal but quits when you remove it, the problem is the diode trio supplying current to the regulator. A jumper from the positive battery terminal to the D+ terminal will get the alternator running normally, but you must disconnect it when you stop the engine to prevent the battery from discharging through the regulator.

EXCITATION

If flashing the field started the alternator, you need to repair the excitation circuit. Excitation current usually comes from the ignition switch or the oil-pressure switch on the engine. It normally passes through an "idiot" light, but sometimes a diode is used instead. The excitation wire usually leads to the D+ or 1 terminal on the alternator, but may also go directly to the regulator.

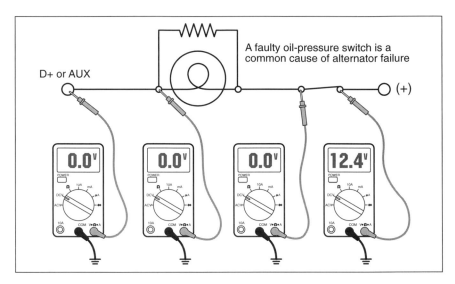

D+ or AUX

A faulty oil-pressure switch is a common cause of alternator failure

(+)

0.0ᵛ   0.0ᵛ   0.0ᵛ   12.4ᵛ

Trace the circuit with your meter. The usual problems are a defective switch or a poor connection. A burned-out warning lamp also will open the excitation circuit if it isn't paralleled with a resistor. In a pinch, use your test light to excite the alternator.

BYPASSING A FAULTY REGULATOR

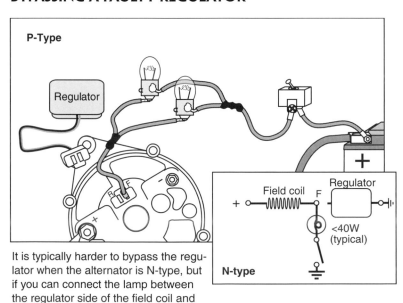

P-Type

Regulator

Field coil   F   Regulator

<40W (typical)

N-type

It is typically harder to bypass the regulator when the alternator is N-type, but if you can connect the lamp between the regulator side of the field coil and the ground, the same principle applies.

If the regulator fails and you don't have a spare, you can operate the alternator without it using your test light to supply the field current. If alternator output is too low, raise it by using a higher wattage bulb—up to about 40 watts—or by connecting a second bulb in parallel. Keep in mind that the alternator is unregulated, so you must make sure not to overload it. If the batteries get warm or start to gas vigorously, disconnect the bulb to turn off the alternator.

DIODES

If the alternator appears to be functioning normally but you are still having charging problems, the problem may be with the diodes.

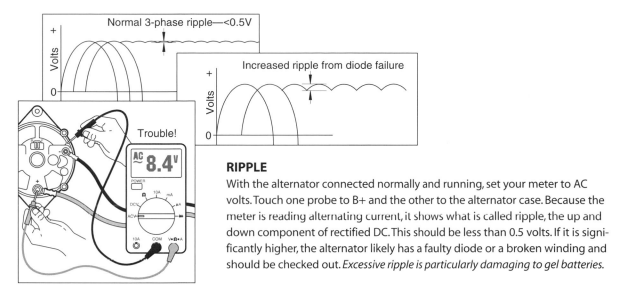

Normal 3-phase ripple—<0.5V

Increased ripple from diode failure

Trouble!

AC 8.4 V

RIPPLE

With the alternator connected normally and running, set your meter to AC volts. Touch one probe to B+ and the other to the alternator case. Because the meter is reading alternating current, it shows what is called ripple, the up and down component of rectified DC. This should be less than 0.5 volts. If it is significantly higher, the alternator likely has a faulty diode or a broken winding and should be checked out. *Excessive ripple is particularly damaging to gel batteries.*

LEAKAGE

Leaking diodes can drain the battery when the alternator is stopped. With the engine not running and the battery switch in the OFF position, disconnect all wires connected to the B+ and the D+ terminals. Set your meter to measure amps and connect it between the positive battery post and B+. The meter will read leakage back through the rectifying diodes. More than a few milliamps means the alternator needs to be serviced. The same test to the D+ terminal shows leakage through the alternator's isolating diodes.

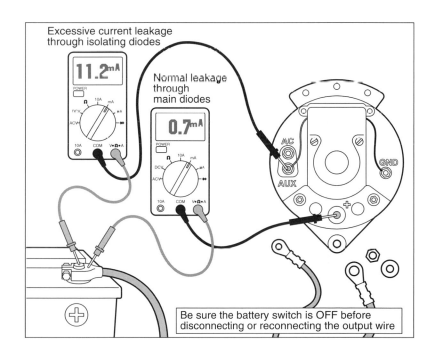

Excessive current leakage through isolating diodes

11.2 mA

Normal leakage through main diodes

0.7 mA

AC

GND

AUX

Be sure the battery switch is OFF before disconnecting or reconnecting the output wire

OPEN OR SHORTED

With the B+ and D+ wires still disconnected, set your meter to the diode-test function and touch the leads to D+ and the AC terminal, then reverse them. If the meter reads less than 1 volt in one direction, O.L in the other, the alternator's isolating diodes are good. Do the same test between B+ and GND to check the main diodes. A reading less than 2 volts in one direction is OK. Similar readings in both directions—either high or low—indicate faulty diodes.

You can also do this test with an ohmmeter, but some have insufficient forward voltage to cause the diode to conduct. If you get an infinite-ohms reading in both directions, try a different meter before condemning the diodes.

DON'T FORGET TO RECONNECT THE OUTPUT CABLE AFTER THESE TESTS!

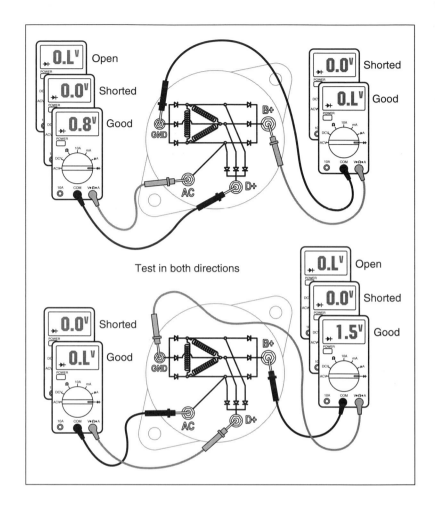

Test in both directions

BATTERY SWITCHING

With a single battery bank, you can wire the alternator output directly to the positive terminal on the battery. Dual battery banks require some method of isolating the banks so they can be used independently.

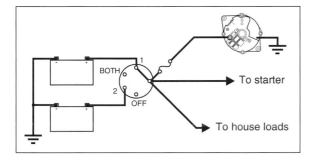

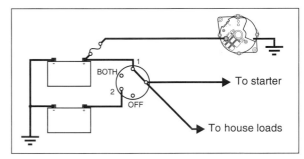

THE STANDARD WAY

Most sailboats are delivered with two batteries connected to a selector switch that allows them to be used independently. For charging, and sometimes for starting, the switch is turned to BOTH. This arrangement has two major flaws. First, if you forget to switch from BOTH when you stop the engine, the starting battery discharges along with the house battery. This is the most common cause of being unable to start the main engine. Second, rotating the switch the wrong way when changing battery selection moves it through OFF rather than BOTH, removing the load from the spinning alternator. This is the most common cause of alternator failure.

DIRECT ALTERNATOR CONNECTION

Connecting the alternator directly to the house battery, not through the selector switch, eliminates the risk of inadvertently removing the load from the alternator, but the switch must still be turned to BOTH to charge the starting battery.

FUSE

ANY WIRE CONNECTED directly to the positive battery terminal, even the output wire from the alternator, must be fused as close to the battery as possible. Otherwise, if the output wire vibrates loose from the B+ terminal on the alternator and comes in contact with the case, the engine, or any other ground, it creates a dead short with a high likelihood of a resultant fire.

ISOLATING DIODES

Inserting isolating diodes into the charging circuit eliminates the risk of alternator damage since the alternator is always connected—through the diodes—to the batteries. And it reduces the risk of leaving the batteries interconnected unless you set the switch to BOTH for starting. But you must still rotate the switch for engine starting, then remember to turn it back or house use will discharge and ultimately damage the starting battery. And unless you modify the charging system, the voltage drop caused by battery isolators will cause chronic undercharging of both batteries.

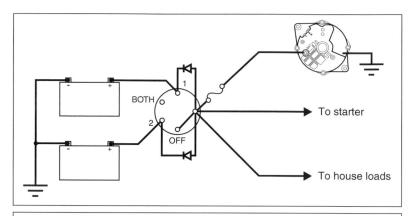

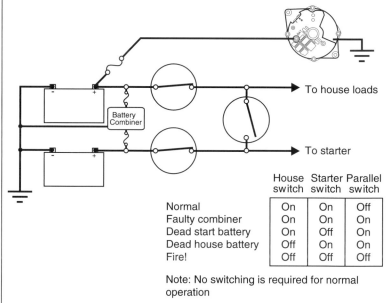

	House switch	Starter switch	Parallel switch
Normal	On	On	Off
Faulty combiner	On	On	On
Dead start battery	On	Off	On
Dead house battery	Off	On	On
Fire!	Off	Off	Off

Note: No switching is required for normal operation

A BETTER WAY

By keeping the starter/starter-battery circuit independent from the house circuit, you never have to change any switch settings while you are aboard. A separate paralleling switch allows the batteries to be combined or substituted in an emergency. The alternator is connected to the house bank. Starting battery charging is accomplished with a battery combiner that connects the batteries when it senses charging voltage—above around 13 volts. Battery combiners cost less than a single alternator repair.

SOLAR CELLS

Solar power is clean, quiet, infinitely renewable, and free—except for the cost of the solar panels. No other form of alternative energy has quite as much appeal. In just 15 minutes the sun bombards the earth with more energy than all of humanity consumes in a year, and the fraction that falls on the on the deck of a 35-foot (11 m) boat is the equivalent of about 600 amp-hours of 12-volt power. All we have to do is convert it from light to electricity.

CHOICES

All solar cells function on the same principle: light striking the top layer of the cell "knocks" electrons into the bottom layer. Connecting the two layers allows the displaced electrons to flow through the circuit and back "home."

CRYSTALLINE

The most efficient silicon-based solar cells are the single-crystal type, where each cell is a single hair-thin wafer sliced like bologna from a "grown" crystal. Polycrystalline cells combine smaller wafers—something like silicon chipboard. This type is only slightly less efficient in ideal light and sometimes better at lower sun angles. For the most output for a given panel size, buy only panels made of crystalline cells.

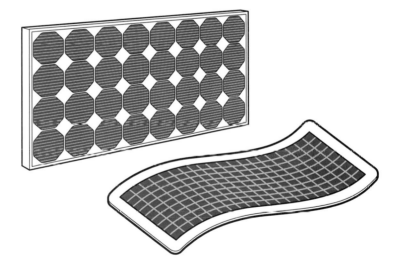

THIN FILM

Amorphous silicon, often called thin film, is like a silicon paint. Widely used in calculators, thin-film solar cells are less than half as efficient as crystalline units. Amorphous silicon can be applied to a flexible stratum to create a flexible panel.

OUTPUT

RATING

Crystalline photovoltaic cells have an open circuit voltage of around 0.5 volts no matter what size they are. Their current output is about 0.25 amps per square inch of cell area. The cells in a panel are connected in series, so their voltages are added together, but the total amperage for the panel is the same as for a single cell. A panel with 36 5-inch (12.7 cm) cells will put out about 5 amps (3.14 x 2.5 x 2.5 x 0.25) at around 18 volts (36 x 0.50). That gives the panel a rating of around 90 watts (18V x 5A).

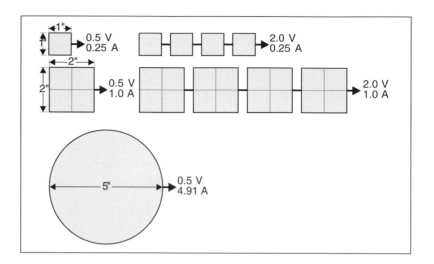

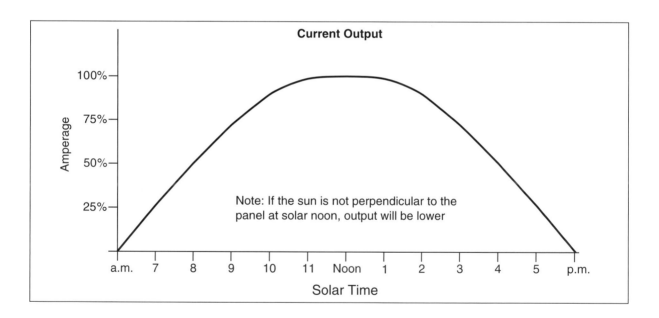

DAILY

Rated output only occurs at high noon; the rest of the time the panel puts out less current. The rule of thumb (for a horizontal panel) is to expect no more than the equivalent of 4 hours of rated output per day. A 5-amp panel should supply about 20 amp-hours daily—when the sun shines.

TEMPERATURE

Solar cells lose efficiency when they get hot. A 10°F (6°C) temperature increase decreases cell voltage about 3%. It is not unusual for cell temperature to exceed 125°F (52°C) in the tropics, reducing actual voltage to about 15% less than the panel's rating (at 77°F, 25°C).

SELF REGULATING

Self-regulating panels have fewer cells—typically 30 to 33—so that their output voltage will be low enough not to require additional regulation. Unfortunately, on a hot day the voltage of a 30-cell panel will fall below 13 volts—too low for appreciable battery charging. Unless you will limit use to a temperate climate, always select panels with more than 33 cells.

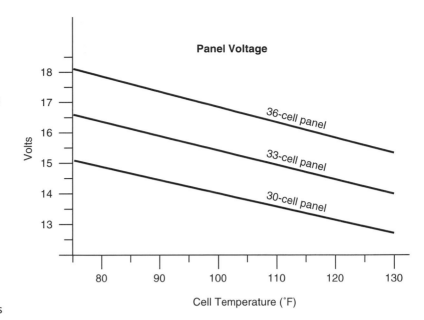

USES

Unrealistic expectations from the current state of solar technology can result in expensive disappointment.

BATTERY MAINTENANCE

If your boat—like most—sits idle for days or weeks, a small solar panel will keep your batteries at full charge and quadruple their life. And unlike a shore-power connection, the solar panel does not introduce any risk of stray-current corrosion (see Chapter 9). The output of a maintenance panel should be about 0.3% of the total battery capacity. For example, for a 220-amp-hour battery bank, you want a panel that puts out about 0.66 amps—close to what you would expect from a 10-watt panel (10W / 16V).

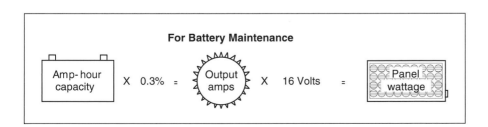

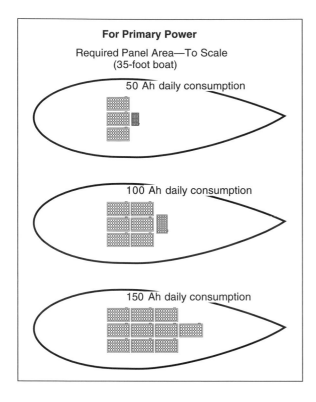

For Primary Power

Required Panel Area—To Scale
(35-foot boat)

50 Ah daily consumption

100 Ah daily consumption

150 Ah daily consumption

PRIMARY POWER SOURCE

With enough solar generating capacity, you could avoid running the engine for electrical power. Unfortunately, a square foot of crystalline solar-panel surface typically generates only about 3 amp-hours per day. In other words, replacing 80 amp-hours of daily consumption (plus 20% battery inefficiency) would require an array roughly the size of a full sheet of plywood. Expect such a solar array to cost more than $2,000. Any attempt to make the sun your primary source of electricity must necessarily be accompanied by a philosophy of power conservation.

INSTALLATION

ORIENTATION

Ashore, solar panels are usually angled toward the track of the sun, but random movement makes a horizontal mount give the best results on a boat not tied to a dock.

LOCATION

Some panels are so shade sensitive that even the thin shadow from a shroud can lower output voltage below battery voltage. Mount panels where they will not be shaded during the peak solar hours.

VENTILATION

It is essential to leave an inch or so of air space beneath panels to avoid output-robbing heat buildup.

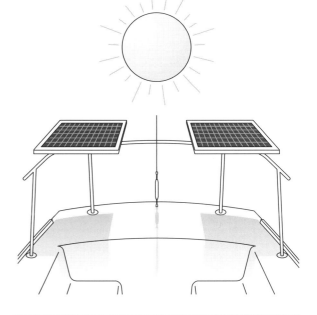

TURNING THE PANEL OFF FOR INSTALLATION

Solar panels start generating as soon as they are exposed to sunlight. To avoid the risk of causing a short circuit, cover the panel during installation to turn it off.

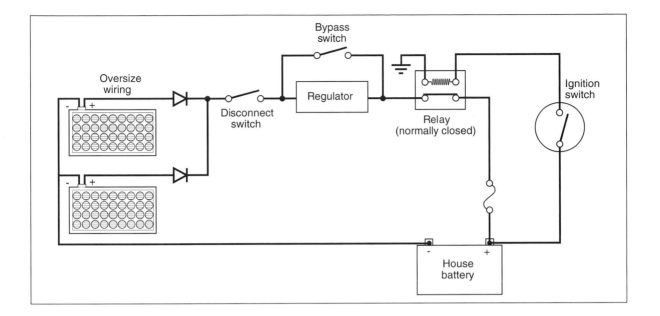

WIRE SIZE

Based on peak output current, connect the panel to the battery with wire one size larger than the formula or 3% table indicates (see Chapter 4). Given the cost of solar panels, you don't want to lose any output to undersize wiring.

COMBINING PANELS

Like batteries, multiple panels are wired in parallel to combine current output.

DIODE

A diode in the + wire lets the solar panel deliver current to the battery, but prevents current from flowing back through the panel at night. A diode for each panel has the added benefit of keep panels isolated in multipanel installations. Diodes do cause a drop in the voltage delivered to the battery—another reason to always select panels with more than 33 cells. Use low-loss Schottky diodes.

FUSE

As mentioned previously, any wire taken directly to the positive side of the battery must be fused as close to the battery as possible. Otherwise, a short in the wire represents a very real fire hazard.

REGULATOR

If the output of the panel exceeds 1% of battery capacity, a regulator is necessary to prevent battery damage. A regulator that disconnects the solar panel when it senses reverse current eliminates the need for a blocking diode.

BYPASS SWITCH

Because they put out a relatively constant current at elevated voltage, solar panels are ideal for equalizing batteries. If you have deep-cycle wet cells, install a bypass switch around the regulator so the full output of the panel can be delivered directly to the battery.

REGULATOR INTERACTION

With the batteries connected to solar panels, the regulator for the alternator may sense elevated voltage in the circuit and turn off the alternator even though the battery is less than fully charged. This can be handled with a manual switch in the + wire of the solar array, or automatically by taking the wire through a normally closed relay energized by the engine ignition switch.

TROUBLESHOOTING

Solar panels are generally trouble-free, another of their many appeals.

VOLTAGE

Check the open-circuit voltage of a new panel in bright sunlight and compare it to the panel's rating. Most manufacturers now warrant output to be within 10% of rating for at least 10 years. If output declines below this threshold, exercise your warranty rights.

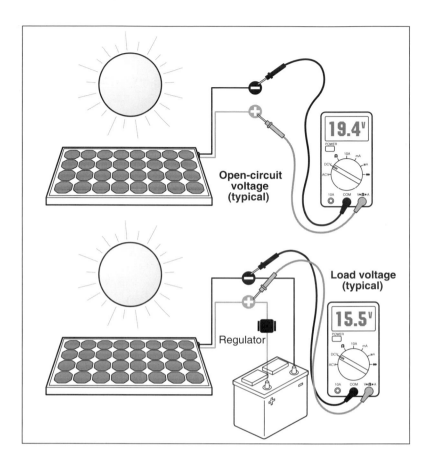

CONNECTIONS

Most solar-panel problems are related to corroded connections. If the panel has a junction box, it is advisable to fill it with silicone sealant after making the initial connections. All other connections should be made below deck.

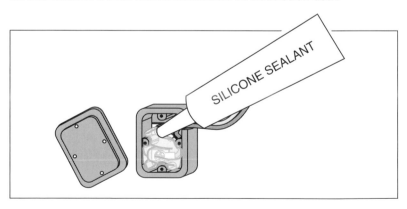

WIND GENERATORS

No charging system seems more compatible with a sailboat than one powered by the wind.

CHOICES

It is instructive to think of wind generators marketed to sailors as falling into one of two categories: the 5-foot-diameter (1.5 m) DC-motor type, and the less obtrusive and less powerful 3-foot-diameter (0.9 m) alternator type. There are, however, now some units that attempt to combine the best features of each type.

Large-diameter wind generators give higher output at all wind speeds, but they may not be left unattended. Sudden squalls have caused many to self-destruct, and even if yours doesn't fly apart, the high output current is likely to damage the generator, wiring, batteries, and other electrical gear. Large-diameter generators require constant vigilance.

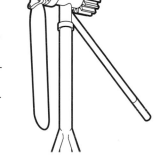

Small-diameter wind generators provide less power, but they may be mounted permanently and more or less ignored. Alternator-type wind generators also require less maintenance. Four-foot (1.2 m) alternator types—providing higher output—are a relatively recent addition to the wind generator arena.

OUTPUT

Wind generator output is related to blade diameter squared and wind speed cubed. In other words, doubling blade diameter quadruples theoretical output (2 x 2); doubling wind speed increases it eight-fold (2 x 2 x 2). The number of blades has no effect on output, but additional blades do tend to reduce noise—a not-insignificant consideration.

RATED OUTPUT

Real output is often quite different from theoretical. The table shows the output you should expect from both 36-inch and 60-inch generators at pertinent wind speeds, regardless of more optimistic output claims from some manufacturers. No wind generator will start at less than 5 knots, and some need 6 or 7 knots of wind to start generating. Above 20 knots, large generators are likely to be shut down due to their high current levels. Some alternator types will also be shut down, switched off automatically to protect their windings from overheating. Given the protected nature of most anchorages, the most meaningful number for comparison is likely to be output at 10 knots of wind speed.

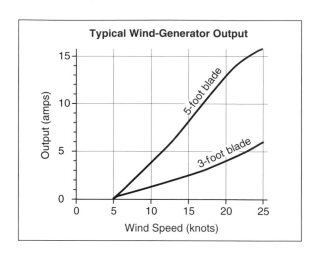

DAILY OUTPUT

Assuming similar efficiencies, the rated output of a 36-inch wind generator will be about 36% of that of a 60-inch unit ($36^2 / 60^2$). But because of the risk of self destruction and damaging high currents, and because it is incredibly dangerous to physically turn an overspeeding generator away from the wind to shut it down, most owners routinely disable large-diameter generators at night and when they are off the boat. The total output of a large-diameter unit limited to 8 hours of daily operation would actually be less than that of an unattended small-diameter unit running around the clock. Where a small-diameter unit can fill daily power requirements, it will be safer and more convenient.

MOUNTING

To maximize output, wind generators must face directly into the wind, which requires a swivel mount. A fixed mount that depends on the weathercocking nature of the boat will be significantly less efficient because boats tend to sail around their anchors and are influenced by currents. And underway, sailboats never sail directly into the wind.

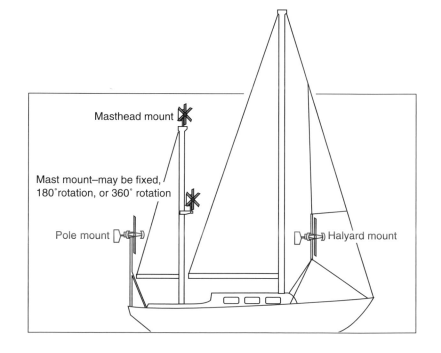

CONNECTIONS

Wind-generator connections are straightforward.

WIRE SIZE

Use the rated output (under load) of the generator to determine the appropriate wire size. Voltage drop should not exceed 3%.

FUSE

As with all direct battery connections, a fuse is required to avoid a fire risk. However, should this particular fuse blow, it unloads the wind generator, which may cause the machine to overspeed and self-destruct. Use the largest-capacity fuse that does not exceed the capacity of the wire. If this is not at least 50% above the maximum generator output, you will need to use larger wire to allow for the use of a higher-rated fuse.

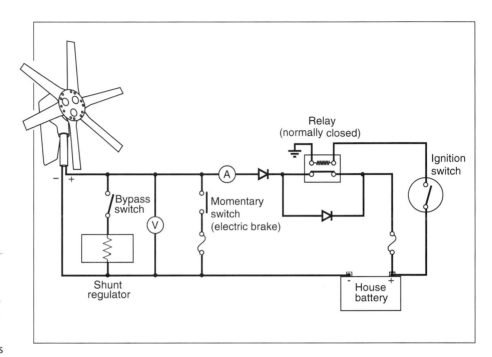

REGULATOR

All wind generators require regulation. Most can be controlled with a shunt-type regulator. This device, connected across the generator circuit rather than in series, diverts current through a resistive load as the voltage in the circuit rises toward a preset limit.

The only available regulation for a few wind generators is to monitor output and shut down the generator when battery voltage reaches 14.4 volts. In anything but light winds, that is likely to leave the battery undercharged.

BYPASS

Shunt regulators begin to divert current from the battery well before the voltage in the charging circuit rises to the preset limit. Output typically starts tapering off at around 13 volts. Disabling the regulator—by switching it out of the circuit—results in faster charging, but battery voltage must be monitored closely and not allowed to rise above 14.4 volts before returning the regulator to the circuit. Otherwise the batteries will suffer serious and permanent damage.

Taking the regulator out of the circuit also lets you use a wind generator to equalize deep-cycle wet cells, provided output from the generator does not exceed 4% of the amp-hour capacity of the batteries.

DIODE

A diode is always required between the generator and the battery. Sometimes the regulator incorporates the diode. This simplifies the connection to a single bank but complicates a dual-bank connection unless the regulator has dual isolated outputs. Make battery connections downstream of any existing isolation diodes to avoid detrimental voltage drop.

REGULATOR INTERACTION

As with solar power, elevated battery voltage due to a wind generator can cause the engine alternator to shut off even though the battery is less than fully charged. Disconnecting the wind generator is usually not an option because it can result in damaging overspeeding. Inserting an extra diode in the wind generator's charging circuit should reduce the generator-induced voltage sufficiently to eliminate interaction problems. Like the automatic disconnect for the solar panel, this can be handled automatically with a normally closed relay connected to the ignition switch.

MONITORING

A voltmeter and an ammeter wired into the charging circuit allows convenient performance monitoring.

TROUBLESHOOTING

Overcharging, under-charging, or a change in performance can lead you to suspect trouble. A few quick tests with your multi-meter will diagnose most wind-generator problems.

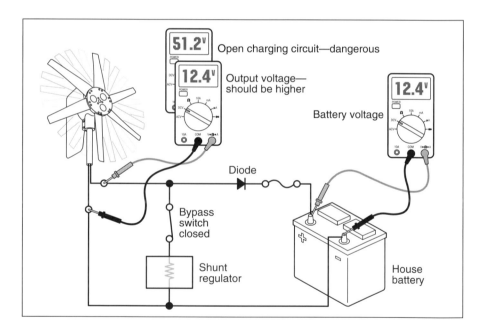

With a diode in the circuit, output voltage with the generator spinning in the wind should be around 0.5 volts above battery voltage. If it is higher, suspect a break in the charging circuit. Be more cautious than usual when checking wind-generator output; the open-circuit voltage of some units can well exceed 50 volts—enough to give you a nasty shock.

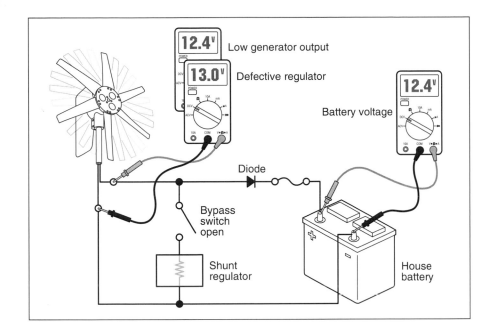

12.4ᵛ Low generator output

13.0ᵛ Defective regulator

Battery voltage **12.4ᵛ**

Diode

Bypass switch open

Shunt regulator

House battery

With generator output confirmed and the generator running, disable or disconnect the regulator and check charging-circuit voltage again. If it is now above battery voltage, the regulator is faulty.

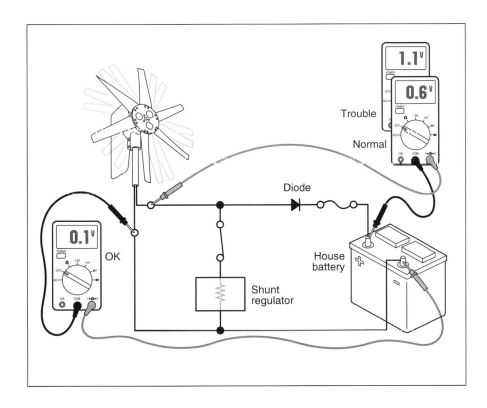

1.1ᵛ Trouble

0.6ᵛ Normal

Diode

0.1ᵛ OK

House battery

Shunt regulator

With the generator still running, check both positive and negative legs of the charging circuit for voltage drop. The diode in the positive leg will cause a drop of around 0.6 volts; more than that indicates unwanted resistance. Check for bad connections, broken wires, or blown fuses. Regulators often have an internal fuse.

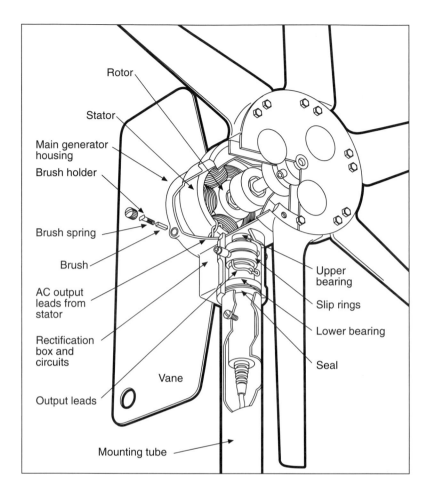

Rotor

Stator

Main generator housing

Brush holder

Brush spring

Brush

AC output leads from stator

Rectification box and circuits

Output leads

Vane

Mounting tube

Upper bearing

Slip rings

Lower bearing

Seal

If the closed-circuit voltage in your initial test was the same as battery voltage, open the charging circuit and check it again to confirm that the generator is not charging. The usual cause of zero output is worn or stuck brushes. Blown diodes are another possibility in alternator-type machines, as is failure of the thermal disconnect in the windings.

WATER GENERATORS

Water generators are essentially wind generators powered by a freewheeling prop as the boat moves through the water. Water's higher density means that water generators are capable of substantial output when a boat is underway. All of the information provided for connecting and testing a wind generator applies equally to water generators.

CHAPTER 8

ALTERNATING CURRENT

N o aspect of sailing is more inherently dangerous than pulling up to a dock and plugging in.

If yours is an older boat, the so-called "shore-power" system was probably just shy of criminal when the boat left the factory, and it hasn't improved with age. Even if your boat is relatively new and wired to the highest standards, the slightest fault—a bit of corrosion or an errant trickle—can put you in grave peril. And let's not overlook the possibility that the last electrician to work on the marina wiring might not have graduated at the top of his class.

Every schoolchild knows electricity and water are a deadly combination. So why would a sailor risk AC power in the wet environment of a boat? Originally, the idea was to take advantage of cheap (and silent) shore power to recharge batteries, provide better cabin illumination at the dock, and perhaps power a small, high-draw appliance like an iron or a coffee-maker. But soon enough boatowners wanted *all* their shoreside comforts and conveniences when they were plugged in. Today's sailors are becoming less willing to give up those conveniences even when they leave the dock.

In this chapter I will show how to wire an onboard AC system for maximum safety. If the AC system on your boat falls short of the standards outlined here, corrective measures are essential. With sufficient care you can make the required changes yourself; AC wiring is no more complicated than DC— only more dangerous. If you decide to take the more prudent course of leaving AC system repairs to a qualified marine electrician, you still should use your multimeter to check your existing AC wiring for the most egregious problems. When it comes to AC power, what you don't know definitely *can* hurt you.

ALTERNATING CURRENT KILLS!

I don't know how to say this any more clearly. It is not just the higher voltage, it is also the pulsating nature of the current. Even a small alternating current, if it passes through your chest, is capable of fatally disrupting heart rhythm. If you accidentally touch a hot AC wire and any part of your body is grounded, you become part of the circuit. If it is your elbow that is grounded, you may escape with nothing worse than a fright and a sore arm muscle, but if the ground connection is at your feet or your other hand, you will be extremely lucky to survive the event. Fortunately it is easy to avoid such a tragedy. Here are the rules:

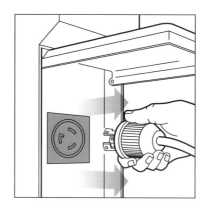

Disconnect the AC system from all power sources. You may have to energize the wiring for testing, but never, ever work on the system hot.

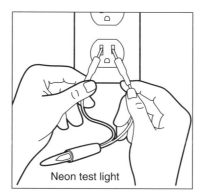

Neon test light

Check all wires with a voltage tester before touching. This practice is the electrician's version of "measure twice, cut once." Use your volt meter or a neon tester, and make sure there is no voltage between any two wires, or any wire and ground. Even if you unplugged the shore-power cord, you may have forgotten to disconnect the inverter.

Keep one hand in your pocket. Obviously you will need both hands occasionally, but the habit of working with one hand until you need the other reduces the risk of lethal shock.

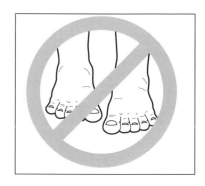

Wear rubber soles. Don't work on the AC system with bare feet. If your sole is damp, you may be electrically connected through a through-hull to ground.

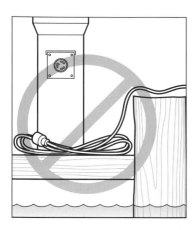

Don't leave the power cord on the dock. A helpful passer-by might plug it back in for you and send you to the next life.

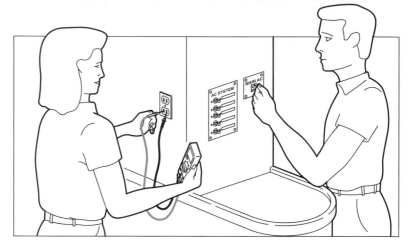

Don't work alone. Especially if you are testing a live circuit, have someone close at hand who can shut off the power and/or provide assistance in case of a shock.

If you keep the danger solidly in mind, working on the AC system can actually be less risky than using it.

AC BASICS

Generators induce a current flow by passing a magnet near a wire coil. But the magnet is spinning, and its opposite pole follows almost immediately, reversing the direction of the induced current. And so it goes. This electron two-step is alternating current.

We can represent AC visually with a wavy line oscillating above and below zero. From peak plus to peak minus and back to peak plus is called a cycle. The frequency of the power is the number of cycles per second, measured in hertz (Hz). In the U.S., AC power has a frequency of 60 hertz.

FREQUENCY

Generated current builds, peaks, then declines as the magnet approaches the wire coil, passes near it, then swings away. As the opposite pole of the magnet passes the coil, current again builds, peaks, and declines, but in the opposite direction.

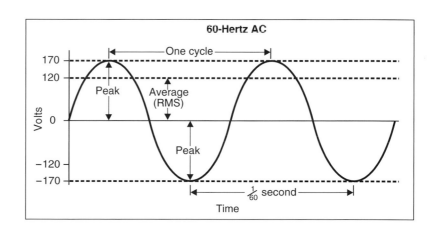

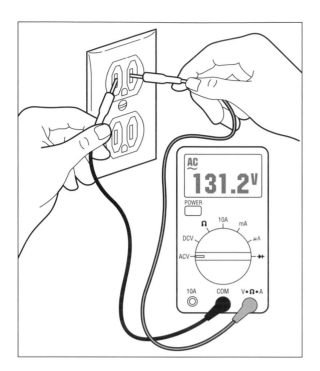

VOLTAGE

Since AC voltage is also oscillating, its designation is actually equivalent DC voltage, called RMS (root mean squared). Like battery voltage, it is subject to some variation.

120 VOLTS

The designation for "standard" household voltage varies from 110 to 125, and the range of actual voltages is even wider. I have adopted 120 volts as the wall-outlet standard in this book, primarily because at exactly ten times 12-volt battery voltage, it simplifies AC-to-DC calculations.

240 VOLTS

Our coverage of AC power does not extend to 240 volts. Two-forty will kill you twice as quickly as 120 volts. If your boat is large enough to require a 240-volt supply, your pockets are deep enough to hire a qualified electrician to work on it for you.

POWER FACTOR

Some components in a circuit, most notably coils, oppose *changes* in current. This isn't resistance as measured by an ohmmeter—it is called *reactance*—but it nevertheless causes many AC components to draw additional current. We account for this by including a *power factor* in AC power calculations, so that $P = V \times I$ becomes $P = V \times I \times PF$, where PF is always 1 or less.

You might expect a 120-volt AC appliance with a 1,200 watt rating to draw 10 amps, but if the PF is 0.5—a common power factor—the actual consumption is 20 amps ($I = P \div [V \times 0.5]$). So the rated wattage of an AC appliance can substantially understate its actual power consumption—an important consideration when sizing wires, inverters, or generators. Sometimes the PF is shown on the faceplate.

THREE-WIRE SYSTEM

In a DC circuit, the wire carrying power from the source to the load is called positive, but with AC voltage switching between positive and negative (relative to ground), we call this side of an AC circuit *hot*. The hot wire in a 120-volt circuit is normally black, but sometimes red or blue.

As with DC, we need a second wire to complete the circuit and provide a return path for the current. This side of the AC circuit we call *neutral*. At the power source, AND ONLY AT THE POWER SOURCE, the neutral side of the circuit is connected to a buried metal plate or bar to hold it at ground potential. The neutral wire is always white.

The third wire is called the *grounding* wire and it, too, is connected to ground *at the power source*. At its other end, the grounding wire is connected to all metal components, junction, and appliance housings and, through the third socket in 120-volt outlets, to the external cases of plug-in equipment. Ashore, the grounding wire is often bare, but in boat wiring it should be insulated and green.

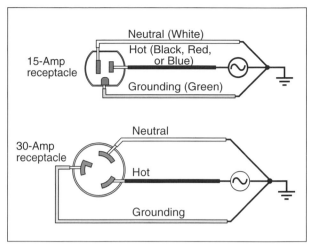

THE GROUNDING WIRE

Since neutral also runs to ground, you might wonder why we need a second grounding wire. It is there to keep you alive. If, for example, wire insulation inside an appliance melts or abrades and the wire comes in contact with the case, it puts the case at the same potential as the hot wire. It doesn't blow a fuse because there is no circuit and thus no current flow. And depending on the fault, it probably doesn't have any effect on the normal operation of the appliance. All seems right with the world ... until you touch the case. Then your body completes the path to ground, and you get a nasty shock.

The grounding wire changes all that. A short to the case instantly becomes a short to ground, probably opening the breaker in the circuit. And even if the short is insufficient to kick the breaker, or if it occurs while you are holding the appliance, the grounding wire still protects you by providing a lower-resistance path to ground than your body does.

Anything that degrades or opens the grounding circuit, such as a corroded or missing ground prong, leaves you dangerously vulnerable. And even if your connections are perfect, marina outlets are far too often poorly grounded or not grounded at all. Before you plug in, check the ground (see Testing later in this chapter).

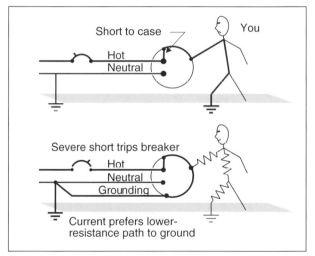

WIRE TYPE AND SIZE

As with DC wiring, use only flexible stranded wire, preferably tinned. In fact, all wiring guidance provided in Chapter 4 applies equally to AC circuits, except that it is primarily amperage capacity and not voltage drop that dictates wire size. If the circuits aboard are protected by 25-amp breakers, #16 AWG (boat cable) is indicated, but as a practical matter, the wire should be a size or two larger than the minimum.

BUNDLING

Gathering parallel wires into bundles is tidy, especially when contained in spiral wrap, but bundling can have unanticipated consequences. Think of too many people in an airless room. Bundled wires combine the heat each generates individually, and for this reason, a wire in a bundle of three should carry not more than 70% of its rated current, 60% in bundles of four to six, 50% in bundles up to 24. A #16-AWG wire in a bundle of eight other wires, for example, should never carry more than 12.5 amps (50% of 25 A).

ALLOWABLE AMPERAGE

Wire Type: AWM, BC5W2, UL1426 Boat Cable
Temperature Rating: 105°C (221°F)

Wire Gauge (AWG)	Outside Engine Space	Inside Engine Space
18	Not allowed *	
16	25	21.3
14	35	29.8
12	45	38.3
10	60	51.0
8	80	68.0
6	120	102

* ABYC guidlines allow limited use of #18 AWG wire inside the panel board, but in deference to human nature, boatowners should never buy wire smaller than #16 AWG.

DERATING FOR BUNDLED AC CABLES

Current-Carrying Conductors	Derating Factor
3	0.7
4 to 6	0.6
7 to 24	0.5
25+	0.4

AT THE DOCK

L ike it or not, *your* AC system begins with the outlet on the dock.

PLUG TYPES

The standard wall outlet is rated at 15 amps. This type of receptacle, called 15-amp straight blade, accepts a common three-blade plug and is still seen at older and smaller marinas. You can also plug a 15-amp plug into a 20-amp straight-blade receptacle, but not vice versa.

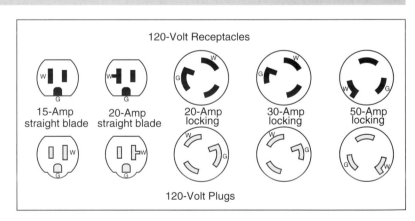

120-Volt Receptacles

15-Amp straight blade | 20-Amp straight blade | 20-Amp locking | 30-Amp locking | 50-Amp locking

120-Volt Plugs

The 30-amp locking receptacle has become the norm at most marinas. Because of this, outfitting your boat to plug into a 30-amp receptacle, even if you don't need 30 amps, will make shore hookups simpler. A locking receptacle makes them more secure.

POLARITY

Since alternating current by definition flows in one direction then the other, reversing the connection has no effect on an AC appliance. But correct polarity is still an essential requirement in AC circuits. Why? When an overload trips the breaker, it disconnects the load from the power. But suppose connections to the dockside receptacle are reversed. That puts the breaker in the neutral side of the circuit, so the circuit is essentially unprotected. The same short now continues uninterrupted until the circuit burns open. If you are lucky, the breaker at the marina office will trip before flames break out, but don't count on it.

Shock risk is also increased. Turning off a breaker appears to remove power from the circuit because it turns off all appliances connected to that circuit. But with reversed polarity you have disconnected the appliance from ground, not from power. THE CIRCUIT IS STILL LIVE.

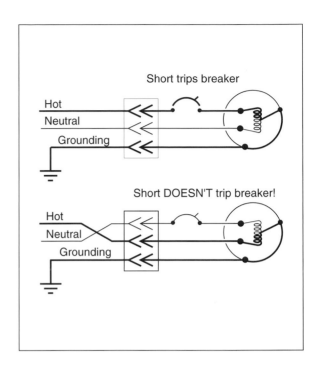

POLARITY TESTER

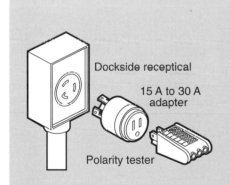

Dockside receptical

15 A to 30 A adapter

Polarity tester

POLARITY TESTER

A POLARITY TESTER hardwired into your AC switch panel (described below) is a good precaution, but if you have an existing circuit fault, damage can occur the instant you plug in. Using a plug-in polarity tester *before* you plug in your power cord is the best way of avoiding reversed polarity. Most also detect an open grounding wire and other dangerous conditions.

The electrical connection between boat and dock is subject to weather, submersion, abrasion, and often strain. It needs to be up to the task.

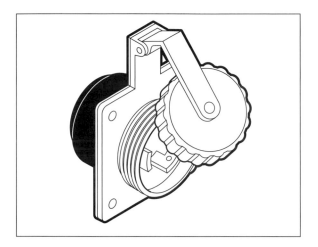

INLET FITTING

The inlet fitting on your boat should be weather tight when connected and when disconnected. Screw-on caps are more secure than those sealed with spring pressure. A high-quality bronze or stainless steel fitting costs only a few dollars more than the plastic variety, but should last the life of the boat.

Locate the inlet where it is convenient but safely out of the way. Mount it as high as possible. The backside of the inlet should be well ventilated and not at risk of mechanical damage.

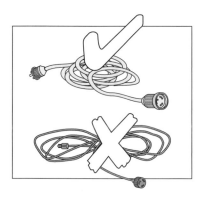

POWER CORD

An extension cord from a builder's supply store, even one labeled "Heavy Duty," is not an appropriate shore-power cord. To stand up to the hard service of marine use, the cable should carry a hard-service rating—SO, ST, or STO. There must be no possibility of the cable pulling free of the plugs (dock cords sometimes become dock *lines*) or of the plugs pulling out of the receptacles. For 30-amp service, the conductors must be #10 AWG or larger.

SUPPLY WIRE

Since protection is somewhere back up the line, wire size to the main breaker is dictated by the type of inlet. A 30-amp inlet requires 10-gauge wire. Fourteen-gauge is adequate for a 15-amp inlet.

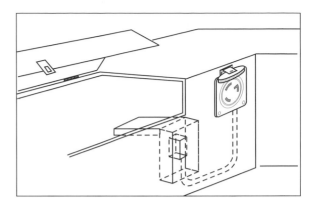

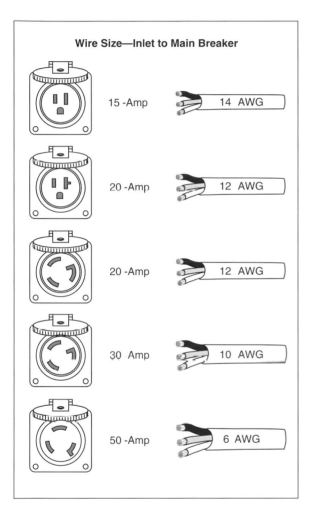

Wire Size—Inlet to Main Breaker

15 -Amp   14 AWG

20 -Amp   12 AWG

20 -Amp   12 AWG

30 Amp   10 AWG

50 -Amp   6 AWG

MAIN BREAKER

Within 10 feet (3 m) (wire distance) of the inlet you must have a circuit breaker that protects both the hot and the neutral conductors. The breaker rating cannot exceed the service; i.e., if you have a 30-amp inlet, the main breaker cannot exceed 30 amps.

Despite the tendency of builders to incorporate the AC main breaker into the main switch panel, locating the breaker in a small (household) breaker box near the inlet fitting—typically high in a cockpit locker—gets it into the circuit sooner and is the preferable configuration. You will rarely, if ever, switch this breaker.

NEUTRAL AND GROUND

A look inside your breaker panel at home will reveal that neutral wires and grounding wires are all connected to the same bus bar. Connecting the neutral wire to the grounding wire on a boat makes the underwater hardware a current-carrying path to ground, an unhealthy circumstance for nearby swimmers. The potential for reversing polarity means appliance cases and wiring boxes might also become energized. On a boat plugged in to shore, the neutral (white) conductor and the grounding (green) conductor MUST NEVER BE DIRECTLY CONNECTED.

AC CIRCUITS

How many AC circuits you need depends on how much AC equipment you have aboard. Keep in mind that you are limited to 30 amps when connected to a 30-amp service.

SINGLE CIRCUIT

The AC requirements on many sailboats can be satisfied with a single circuit. Here, a single double-pole breaker feeds six outlets wired in parallel. Because the outlets are rated for 15 amps, the breaker must also be a 15-amp unit. A single circuit offers the benefit of simplicity, and if (as recommended above) the breaker is located in a dedicated box adjacent to the inlet, this configuration also maintains complete separation between the AC and DC system. No switch panel in the cabin is needed.

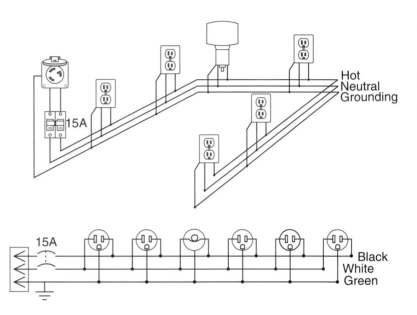

DUAL CIRCUIT

Dual 15-amp circuits let you take full advantage of a 30-amp service. The main breaker is 30 amps, the two circuit breakers 15 amps. All three breakers are located in a box near the power inlet. Here, one circuit supplies a hard-wired battery charger.

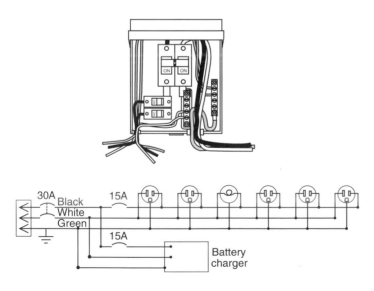

BREAKERS

Although single-pole breakers are commonly used for branch circuits, this is risky economy. Double-pole breakers, which open both sides of the circuit when tripped, fully protect the circuit even if polarity is reversed. Perhaps *you* will never forget to check polarity before plugging in, but *I'm* not that confident.

Breakers should be sized for the wire or for the load, whichever is smaller. For cabin outlet circuits (using at least #16 AWG wire) use 15-amp breakers. If you install 20-amp outlets, the breaker must likewise be 20 amp. For dedicated circuits, a smaller breaker provides some protection for the appliance, but be sure you know the load. This is where the power factor mentioned above comes in. Also, motors and incandescent lights require momentary start-up currents (called inrush) that can be as much as seven times operating currents. Breakers are time-delayed to handle momentary inrush without tripping, but since the delay is related to the percentage of overload, inrush can trip a breaker that is too small.

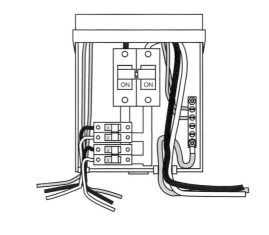

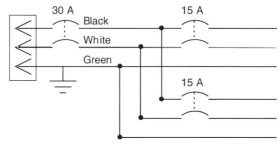

SWITCH PANEL

If you prefer a switch panel in the cabin, commercial units are available. Do not combine AC and DC in a single panel.

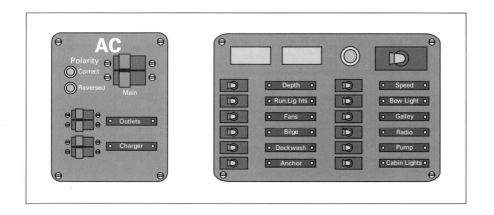

POLARITY TESTER

Your AC system must have a hard-wired reverse-polarity indicator if the circuits are protected with single-pole breakers, but even if you follow the more prudent course of using only double-pole breakers, do not omit this extra safeguard. Reversed polarity still puts ON-OFF switches on the wrong side of the circuit, leaving OFF appliances fully energized. You must know about reversed polarity, and you must correct it.

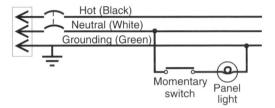

A light or buzzer connected across the white and green wires will not operate as long as the white wire is at 0 potential, but reversing the polarity puts the white wire at 120 volts, illuminating the light or sounding the buzzer. However, since the white and green wires on a boat must never be directly connected, a momentary switch is a required part of the circuit.

An alternative method of maintaining the required separation between white and green is to use a high-resistance indicator like a neon lamp. The circuit shown allows the indicators to operate without manual intervention, and with a resistance exceeding 25,000 Ω, the potential current is less than 5 mA, too little to cause any mischief. This type of polarity indicator is required if your AC circuits are protected by single-pole breakers.

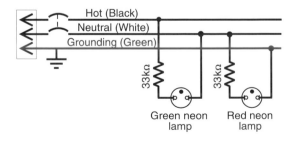

ROUTING AC WIRING

AC wiring should never be routed where it might be at risk of submersion. The best place for AC wiring is high in the boat—against the underside of the deck. Do not bundle AC wiring with DC wiring. There is considerable potential to confuse the black AC hot conductor with the DC negative—also black—so strive to keep the wiring separated and clearly labeled. (For new DC wiring, use yellow wire for the negative.) As with DC wiring, support the wire continuously with conduit, or at least every 18 inches (0.5 m) with cable clamps or wire ties. Protect the wiring from chafe.

JUNCTION BOXES

All AC connections must be protected by an enclosure. Wires should enter junction, outlet, and breaker boxes from the bottom so they cannot provide an entry path for water. Clamp the wire where it enters the box to avoid the risk of chafe from the motion of the boat. Leave enough extra wire (around 4 inches) in outlet boxes to allow the outlet to be connected outside the box. Fold the excess wire behind the outlet.

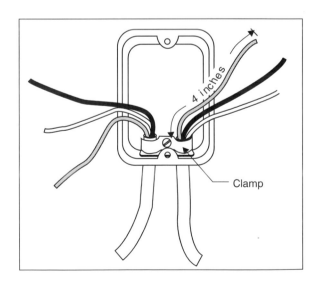

OUTLETS

"HI HO SILVER"

The Lone Ranger's famous call to his white horse has long provided the association necessary for me to remember which wire connects to which terminal on a polarized outlet. *White* goes to *silver*. The black wire connects to the opposite terminal, usually brass, but sometimes dark. The green terminal is for the green grounding wire.

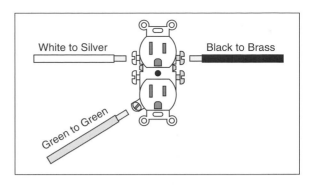

WIRE TERMINALS

Ashore, outlet terminal screws are simply tightened onto a loop of wire. This is inadequate on a boat both because the wire is stranded, not solid, and because boats introduce motion into the equation. As with all connections, those to outlets (and other terminal screws) require a proper terminal on the conductor. Where the terminal screws are captive, use locking spade terminals rather than ring terminals. You can connect wire directly to commercial-grade outlets that have screw-tightened wire clamps.

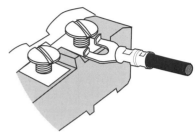

GROUND FAULT INTERRUPT

Regular circuit breakers are essentially fire-protection devices and offer no protection against electrical shock. A ground-fault circuit interrupter (GFCI), on the other hand, provides a high degree of shock protection. If you accidentally touch an energized wire or component and you are grounded, the GFCI disconnects the circuit in about 1/40 of a second, too little time for the current to build to a dangerous level. In recognition of the increased risk of shock in damp environments, many municipal building codes mandate GFCIs in bathrooms and, increasingly, kitchens. Boats are damp environments, and every outlet on a boat should be protected by a GFCI.

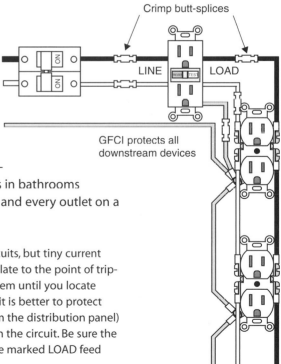

It is possible to install a GFCI in the main panel to protect all circuits, but tiny current leaks that are inevitable in the marine environment can accumulate to the point of tripping the GFCI. And the tripped GFCI disables your entire AC system until you locate these nearly undetectable leaks. To minimize nuisance tripping, it is better to protect each circuit individually. Replacing the first outlet (counting from the distribution panel) with a GFCI outlet protects the rest of the downstream outlets in the circuit. Be sure the wires marked LINE are connected to the power source and those marked LOAD feed the remainder of the circuit.

THE GREEN-WIRE CONTROVERSY

Should any of the various metal cases enclosing your AC system become energized, the green wire provides a low-resistance path to ground. But what if the leak is into the DC wiring, caused, for example, by a crossed wire or a short in a dual-voltage appliance (charger, inverter, dual-voltage light fixtures)?

THE DANGER

Any AC that leaks into the DC system will seek ground, meaning it will automatically travel through the wiring to the ground connection on the engine and down the prop shaft to the water. (If you have a flexible shaft coupling, you need a shaft brush to make electrical contact with the shaft.) This is essentially the same as dropping a hot wire into the water. In freshwater, this poses a real risk of electrocution for anyone in the water nearby. The better conductivity of salt water (which tends to pass the current straight down to ground) reduces the risk of electrocution, but the current field can be (and has been) enough to paralyze muscles and cause a swimmer to drown.

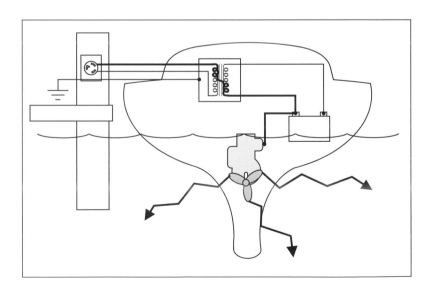

GROUNDING THE GREEN WIRE

To reduce the risk to swimmers, the green wire should be connected to the ground terminal on the engine. This gives AC leakage into the DC system a safe path to ground. But you must be aware that grounding the green wire is not without problems. Should the green wire have a fault somewhere between the power inlet and the buried grounding plate, ground-fault current will flow into the water—just what we are trying to prevent. So it is essential to test the ground *at the dock,* and to keep cords and plugs in good condition. Protecting all AC circuits with GFCIs virtually eliminates this risk.

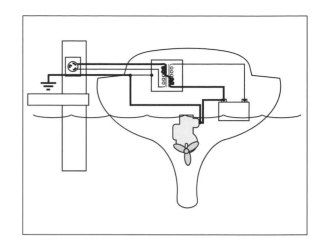

GALVANIC CORROSION

A more insidious problem is galvanic corrosion. Connecting the green wire to an underwater fitting completes the circuit between your boat and all other nearby boats with their own green wires grounded. With seawater as the electrolyte, every grounded fitting essentially becomes part of a big battery.

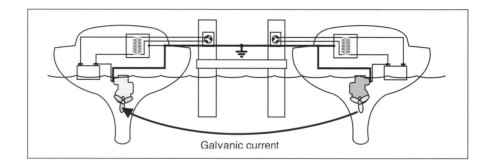

Galvanic current

If your fittings are less noble on the galvanic scale than your neighbors' (see Chapter 9), they are anodes and begin to erode. This can be bad news if you have an aluminum outdrive in the water and your neighbors' underwater fittings are bronze and stainless steel.

STRAY-CURRENT CORROSION

Even if your prop and shaft are similar to those around you and well protected with zinc, stray DC currents from a neighboring boat can seek ground through your green-wire connection, causing electrolysis. A serious stray-current leak can eat underwater components away in a matter of hours. Boats sink at the dock every year due to this condition.

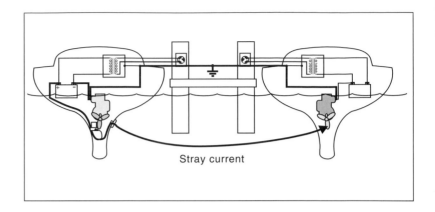

Stray current

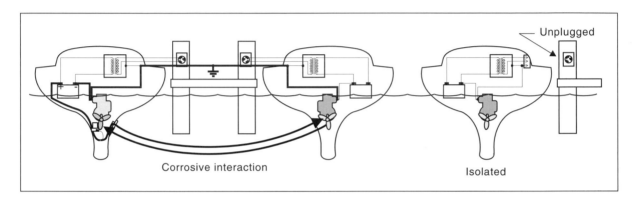

Corrosive interaction

Isolated

Unplugged

CUTTING THE GREEN WIRE

Disconnecting the green wire from the ground lug on the engine eliminates the risk of galvanic or stray-current caused by other boats. But it puts anyone in the water at risk while the boat is plugged in. Don't do it. There are safer solutions.

UNPLUG

Unplugging the boat breaks the grounding wire connection, minimizing or eliminating the risks of galvanic and stray-current corrosion caused by other boats. It also removes the risk to swimmers. Unplug when anyone is going in the water near the boat, and always leave the boat unplugged when you are not aboard. (A solar panel is better for your batteries than a battery charger anyway.)

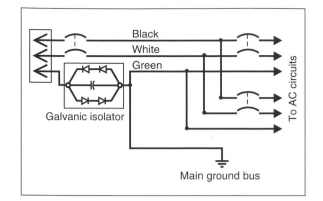

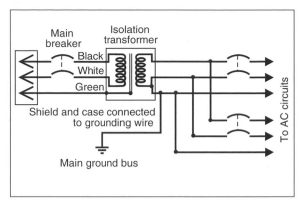

GALVANIC ISOLATOR

The galvanic isolator is simply a pair of diodes connected in parallel to a second pair conducting in the opposite direction. Since it takes about 0.6 volts to "push the gate open" (i.e., cause a diode to become conductive), two diodes in series block all current flow unless the voltage exceeds about 1.2 volts. Galvanic voltages between underwater metals are lower than this, so no current flows. The voltage of most stray currents, by the time it reaches your boat through the water, will also be too low to cause the diodes to pass a current. Opposing pairs of diodes pass current in both directions, so both AC and DC flows freely through the isolator once the diodes become conductive. Galvanic isolators need hefty diodes able to carry short-circuit amperage—up to 3,000 amps in a 30-amp circuit—long enough for the circuit breaker to trip. Unfortunately, not all isolators have this capability. Some isolators parallel a capacitor—an electronic component that passes AC but not DC—so that a diode failure does not disconnect the grounding wire, a potentially hazardous condition.

Insert the galvanic isolator into the green wire as soon as it comes aboard to prevent unknown connections between the AC grounding wire and the DC system from allowing currents to bypass the isolator.

ISOLATION TRANSFORMER

Shore power flowing through one side of an isolation transformer induces AC power on the other side that energizes the boat's AC system, but there is no direct electrical connection between the boat's AC system and shore. The DC system is likewise isolated from shore, eliminating external galvanic and stray-current corrosion as effectively as unplugging. Isolation transformers also eliminate most polarity concerns, but because they are big, heavy (200 lb.), and expensive, they are rarely installed on modest sailboats.

A few quick tests with your multimeter will help you assess the condition of your AC system.

POLARITY

We never think about polarity ashore, but its importance in the wet environment cannot be overemphasized. Not only must you verify the polarity of every dock connection, but if the polarity of any outlet is reversed, the shock risk of any appliance plugged into that outlet increases. Check all outlets for correct polarity, even those you didn't wire (perhaps especially those).

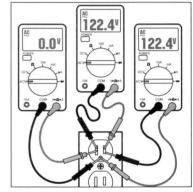

Check polarity with your voltmeter by measuring the voltage between the receptacle's long socket (neutral) and the roundish grounding socket. The meter should read zero. Checked across the short socket (hot) and the grounding socket, the voltage should be normal—around 120 volts. It is a good practice to confirm the neutral connection by also measuring the voltage between the short and long sockets. BE SURE YOU DO NOT TOUCH THE METAL PART OF THE METER PROBES WHEN MAKING THESE TESTS.

You can perform these same tests with a neon test lamp. When the lamp lights, it shows a voltage differential; when it fails to light, both sockets (or wires) are at the same potential. A plug-in polarity tester is the easiest of all to use: just plug it into each outlet.

GROUNDING WIRE

If you have a generator or inverter, shut off the former, disconnect the latter, and switch both out of the AC circuit. Unplug your shore-power cord from the dock—but not from the boat—and take the plug into the cabin. If you have a galvanic isolator—or if you aren't sure—insert the stripped end of a short piece of insulated wire into the ground socket of a cabin outlet and touch the other end to the ground blade on the plug. This discharges the capacitor in the isolator (if it has one). Set your meter to measure resistance (Ω) and touch one probe to the ground blade on the plug and the other to the grounding socket of the outlet. If you don't get a near-zero reading, the ground is faulty and must be fixed. Check the ground connection of every onboard outlet this way.

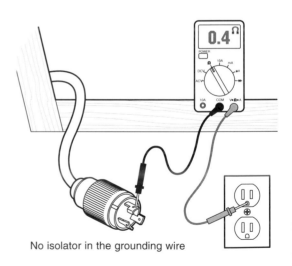

No isolator in the grounding wire

ISOLATED GROUND

In the previous test, a galvanic isolator in the circuit increases the resistance measured by the meter. The meter may take a few minutes to stabilize because the voltage from the meter is recharging the capacitor. When the meter settles, note the reading. Remove the meter and discharge the capacitor again by shorting the ground blade to a ground socket. With the meter connections reversed, recheck the resistance, again allowing time for the reading to stabilize. If both readings are about the same and above 50 ohms, the isolator checks out. If the meter reads O.L or near zero in either direction, the isolator is defective.

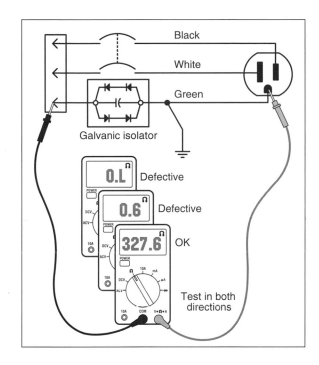

If your meter has a diode-test setting, the same test on this meter setting should give a reading of around 1.0 volt in both directions. A reading of around 0.5 volts indicates a shorted diode; 0.0 volts means tandem diodes are shorted. An O.L reading tells you the diodes are open. Shorted diodes render the isolator ineffective. Open diodes break the grounding connection, a dangerous condition that must not be allowed.

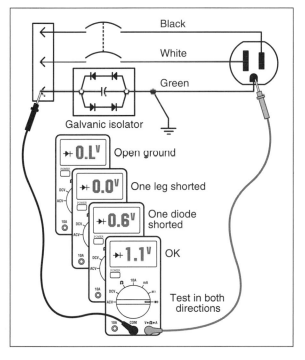

GREEN-WIRE CONNECTION

To verify a good green-wire connection, measure the resistance between the ground blade on the plug and the negative battery cable. It should be near zero (or whatever resistance your isolator exhibited in the previous test).

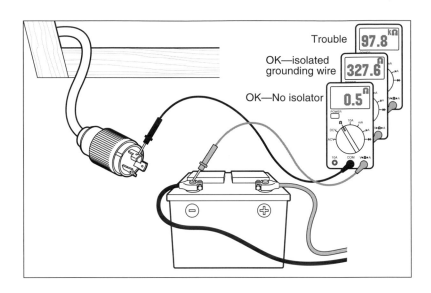

GROUND AND NEUTRAL SEPARATION

Make sure the shore-power cord is unplugged, generators and inverters are off *and* switched out of the AC circuit, and all AC breakers are in the ON position. Double-check for voltage in the system by inserting your voltmeter probes into the slots of any outlet. Check between hot and neutral, between hot and ground, and between neutral and ground. Now switch the meter to ohms (Ω) and measure the resistance between neutral and ground. The meter should read O.L if you do not have a hard-wired polarity tester in the system, above 25,000 ohms (25 kΩ) if you do. A low resistance reading means neutral and ground are tied together. This connection *must* be located and eliminated.

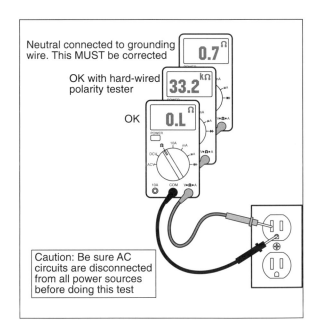

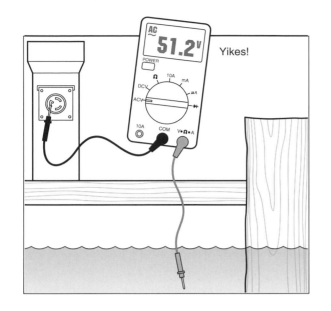

GROUND FAULT

Set your meter to AC volts and insert one probe into the grounding socket of the dockside outlet. WARNING: THE GROUNDING SOCKET IS EASY TO IDENTIFY IN 15-, 20-, AND 30-AMP RECEPTACLES, BUT LESS OBVIOUS IN 50-AMP RECEPTACLES. BE SURE YOU *KNOW* WHICH IS THE GROUNDING SOCKET. Dangle the other probe into the water. Any voltage reading indicates a serious grounding leak and condemns the outlet.

STRAY CURRENT

After checking for a grounding leak, reset the meter to the highest DC amp setting, and check for DC current between the grounding outlet and the water, switching down as necessary. Any reading above around 10 mA suggests stray current from nearby boats and you should not connect to this outlet unless your AC system is isolated.

LEAKAGE

With your shore-power cord plugged into the boat but not into the dock (generators and inverters off and disconnected), make sure there is no AC voltage between the grounding socket in the dock receptacle and the grounding blade on the cord plug. Set the meter to the highest DC amp setting, switching down as necessary. Any current that passes through the meter is leakage. If the current is flowing toward the boat (a + reading with the red probe to the receptacle, black to the plug), it is damaging your underwater fittings; if it flows the other way, the fittings on neighboring boats are suffering. A galvanic isolator in the grounding wire should block all galvanic current and your meter should read zero (although some isolators pass a few milliamps, which zinc anodes should easily handle). If the meter reads more than 15 mA, the isolator is not preventing corrosion.

INVERTERS

An inverter, functioning like a battery charger in reverse, allows AC appliances to be powered by the ship's batteries. Advancing technologies have made inverters more efficient and more affordable. They have become an extremely popular add-on in recent years.

TYPES

Line-frequency inverters are usually bigger and always heavier than equivalent *high-frequency* inverters. In the past, line-frequency inverters enjoyed a lower failure rate, but today dependability is more a function of the quality of the inverter than of the number of electronic components it contains. The line-frequency inverter's primary advantage has long been its "reversibility," becoming a powerful battery charger, but small inverters (under 1,000 watts) nearly all use high-frequency switching. High-frequency switching is finding its way into high-power inverters, including inverter/charger models.

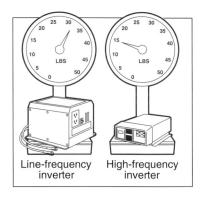

Line-frequency inverter   High-frequency inverter

WAVEFORM

Inverters that generate true sine-wave power are more expensive than those that have a square waveform, but the price difference is narrowing. The power from a sine-wave inverter is indistinguishable from shore power, so it will run any appliance. Most AC equipment will also run fine on square-wave AC, particularly the stepped square wave (called *modified sine wave*) inverters typically generate. But some appliances, notably microwaves, televisions, laser printers, variable-speed devices, and battery chargers (for ni-cads) can have problems with square-wave power and may even be damaged. Before you buy an inverter, know what you want it to power.

SIZING

Inverters are typically most efficient at about two-thirds rated capacity, so select an inverter with a continuous-output rating of about 50% more than the wattage of the appliances you want the inverter to power. Be sure it has adequate surge capacity to handle start-up loads.

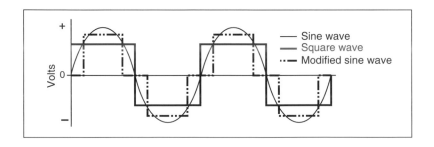

LOAD REALITIES

Often overlooked in selecting an inverter is the load it places on the ship's batteries. A 120-volt AC appliance draws 10 times the rated amps when it is running on 12 volts, plus additional amps to run the inverter. The actual draw is further affected by the PF of the appliance and the effect of the inverter's waveform.

For example, a microwave oven rated at 700 watts would seem to draw 5.8 amps, but with a PF of around 0.6, the actual draw is closer to 10 amps at 120 volts. In addition, microwave ovens don't much like square-wave power, so they are about 30% less efficient when powered by a square-wave (modified sine-wave) inverter. That means the inverter has to deliver 13 amps—1,500 watts—to power the oven. A 1,500-watt draw on a 12-volt battery results in 125-amp current. But the inverter is only about 85% efficient, so the actual draw is closer to 150 amps. This likely exceeds starter-motor draw, so if you run this microwave for 15 minutes, the effect is similar to cranking the engine for that long.

Small inverters are a marvelous convenience, but large inverters will quickly overwhelm your batteries unless their draw is offset by concurrent replenishment, meaning that you will normally need to run the engine while the inverter is under significant load.

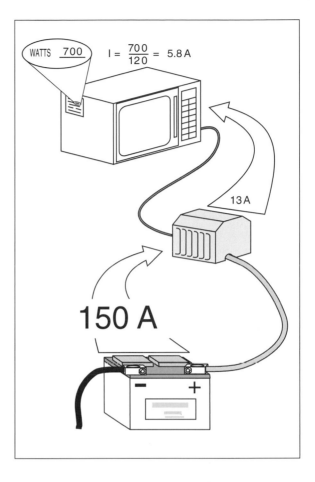

$$\text{WATTS} \quad \underline{700} \qquad I = \frac{700}{120} = 5.8\,A$$

13 A

150 A

BATTERY CAPACITY

THE AMP-HOUR DRAW from a 1,500-watt inverter load for 15 minutes (plus inefficiency) is "only" 37.5 Ah, but you will recall from Chapter 4 that a high discharge rate severely reduces battery capacity. A discharge rate of 150 amps for 15 minutes will leave a 200 Ah battery (20-hour rating) close to 50% discharged. In all likelihood, such a heavy draw will pull battery voltage below 10.5 volts in less than 15 minutes and trip the inverter's low-voltage shutdown switch. The actual amount of battery capacity needed to support an inverter ultimately depends how much you use it between battery charges, but limiting inverter wattage to five times battery capacity is a good rule of thumb. In other words, don't expect a 100 Ah battery to power an inverter larger than 500 watts.

CONNECTIONS

PORTABLE

Small inverters have the AC outlet built into the unit, avoiding a direct connection to the AC system. Most are equipped with a cigarette-lighter plug, but with a current limit of 15 amps. Such plugs are inappropriate for inverters larger than 150 watts. Even then you must make sure that the wire from the battery to the socket is of adequate size. For example, a round-trip wire length of 20 feet (6 m) requires 10-gauge wire.

Unless you absolutely need the portability of a plug, remove it and wire even a small inverter directly to the battery or the distribution panel. WARNING: FEW INVERTERS ARE PROTECTED AGAINST REVERSE POLARITY. IF YOU REVERSE THE CONNECTIONS TO THE BATTERY, YOU WILL RUIN THE INVERTER. The center contact on the plug is positive, so be sure to label the wire when your remove the plug. As with all direct connections to the battery, a fuse in the positive line is an essential safeguard.

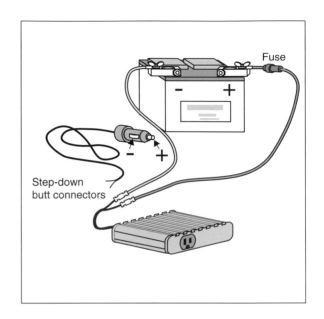

CONSOLE

Large inverters are always wired directly to the battery (or adjacent distribution posts). A slow-blow fuse must be included in the positive side of the DC connection. Wire size must be adequate (see Chapter 4); for example, a 2,500-watt inverter less than 5 feet (1.5 m) from the batteries requires size 1/0 cable.

Inverters without built-in AC receptacles nearly always include an internal transfer switch to prevent the inverter from being on line when the AC system is energized from another source. If you wire the inverter to outlets and appliances that are also connected to the shore-power inlet or a generator, and the inverter does not have a transfer switch, you must install one.

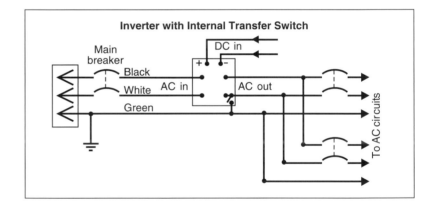

LOCATION

AN INVERTER SHOULD IDEALLY BE LOCATED adjacent to the batteries, but never inside the battery compartment. The mounting location must be dry, and since inverter efficiency declines as the temperature of the unit rises, good ventilation is another requirement. In the tropics a cooling fan will improve both output and reliability.

TRANSFER SWITCH

The transfer switch makes certain that only one source of AC power can be connected to your AC circuits at a time. A low-tech way of accomplishing this is to feed inverter (and generator) output to a cord that fits the shore-power inlet. Since only one cord can be plugged in at a time, the AC wiring can never be connected to more than one source. The transfer switch accomplishes the same thing, only more conveniently.

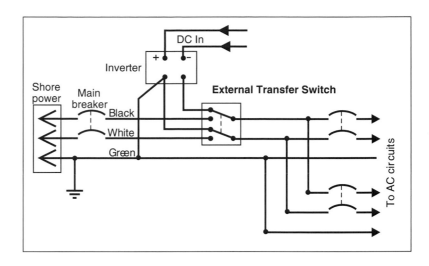

NEUTRAL AND GROUNDING CONNECTION

We saw earlier that the neutral and grounding wires are connected together only at the power source, never on the boat. In the case of shore power, the power source is the breaker panel servicing the dockside outlet. But what happens when the power source is an inverter or a generator on the boat? For shock protection it remains essential to have the neutral and grounding wires connected together at the power source. But whenever the power source is not on the boat, this connection must be broken. This is a second function of the transfer switch—to open the connection between neutral and ground when the boat is connected to shore power.

For heavy or prolonged AC loads away from the dock, the only practical solution is a generator. Plugging the dock cord into the outlet of a portable generator is the easiest way to connect it to cabin outlets. Gensets installed below deck are sufficiently expensive and complicated that professional installation is usually prudent.

TRANSFER SWITCH

It must be impossible for the generator and shore power (or the inverter) to feed the AC circuits at the same time. This is commonly accomplished by running shore power through the inverter's internal transfer switch, with a second break-before-make transfer switch downstream to select the genset. A three-way transfer switch is another alternative.

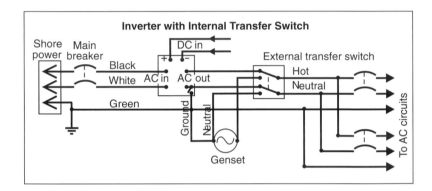

Inverter with Internal Transfer Switch

FREQUENCY

Generator output voltage should be within a few volts of 120, and frequency should be close to 60 Hz. You can measure voltage with your multimeter, but how do you monitor frequency? With a half-dozen components available from your local Radio Shack, you can make a simple frequency meter.

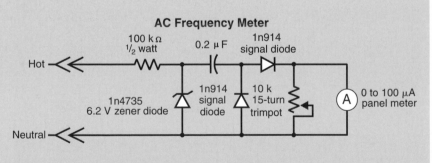

AC Frequency Meter

To calibrate it, connect it to shore power and adjust the trimpot until the ammeter reads exactly 60 μA. The meter reading will now correspond to the line frequency. (For a full explanation of how this circuit works, see *Boatowner's Illustrated Handbook of Wiring* by Charlie Wing.)

CHAPTER 9

HEAVEN AND EARTH

There is an old joke about a man standing in the middle of a park blowing a single braying note on a beat-up trumpet. When the police arrive, they ask him what he is doing.

"Keeping the elephants away," the man says.

"But sir, there are no elephants within thousands of miles," the officer points out.

"See," replies the man.

Lightning protection is like that. If you take preventative measures and your boat never gets struck, at least you can say, "See." But there is an absence of scientific evidence that anything improves the odds of being spared a strike.

Don't flatter yourself that you can be a cosmic player: lightning doesn't know you exist, and it doesn't care. The trick to dealing with lightning is the same as with elephants: stay out of the way. On a sailboat, staying out of the way primarily means giving the lightning an unimpeded path to ground.

A good ground is also required by onboard radios to provide a counterpoise for long-distance transmissions. In this chapter we detail a grounding system that reduces the risk of damage and injury from a lightning strike and simultaneously serves as a radio counterpoise. Bonding, a second component of lightning protection, is also covered.

LIGHTNING PROTECTION

Despite the low risk, statistically, of being struck by lightning, getting caught out on the water in an electrical storm can be a frightening event. Fortunately, going below provides the crew substantial protection. It is the boat that is in greater peril. The best way to minimize the risk of damage is with a properly configured lightning-protection system.

LIGHTNING ROD

The lightning rod was conceived in 1752 by Ben Franklin to protect wooden structures from fire by attracting the lightning strike and conducting it safely to ground. Lightning that would otherwise strike nearby finds the rod and its ground cable a lower resistance path to ground than another 100 feet (30 m) of air or the roof of a wooden building.

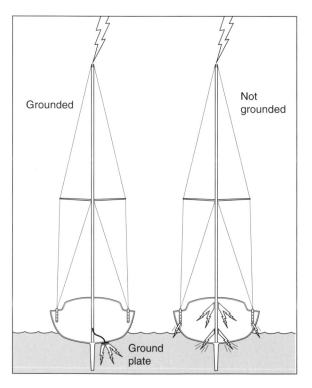

A sailboat with an aluminum mast already has a conductor sticking up in the air. The only thing necessary to make it a lightning rod is to give it a good ground, but the concept of *attracting* lightning makes some sailors reluctant to ground the mast. This logic is fundamentally flawed because, grounded or not, an aluminum mast is a better conductor than air and thus attractive to nearby lightning. When a hitchhiking strike reaches the bottom of an ungrounded mast, it generally fires through the hull to the water, often leaving holes big enough to sink an untended boat. It may also leap to other metal components in the boat, potentially passing through a crewmember.

There is compelling evidence that grounding the mast lowers the incidence of damage or injury from a lightning strike, and no evidence that it increases the likelihood of being struck.

STATIC DISSIPATOR

Some would have you believe that topping your mast with a pointed rod or a copper bottle brush will prevent a lightning strike. The theory is that the point or points of these static dissipators bleed off the charge from the grounded mast, thus lowering the voltage differential below what is required to "spark" lightning. Dissipators do bleed off static charge, but, to use a cliché, there is plenty more where that came from. Trying to bleed the ocean's charge into the air with a dissipator on your mast is like trying to lower the ocean's level with a soda straw. Ironically, because a dissipator ionizes the air around it, under some circumstances it could theoretically contribute to a lightning strike, although it is extremely doubtful that these units have any effect either way.

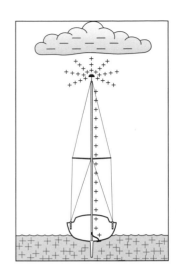

CONE OF PROTECTION

Intuitively, a mast sticking up would seem to put you at greater risk during an electrical storm, not unlike standing beneath the only tree on a golf course. However, powerboaters are statistically at much greater personal risk. If your mast is grounded, it is actually your savior. When the mast is closer than the ground, lightning tends to divert to it. This results in a cone-shaped area that is essentially protected from lightning. This area is known as the cone of protection. It has a height and radius approximately equal to the mast height.

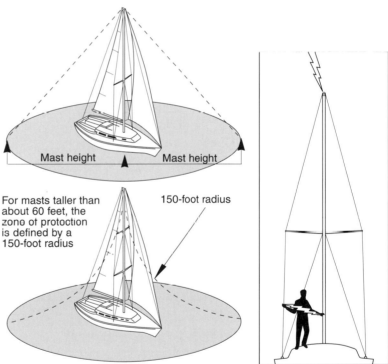

For masts taller than about 60 feet, the zone of protection is defined by a 150-foot radius

150-foot radius

As long as the boat is entirely within the cone, there is little risk of anyone aboard being struck directly. However, you are still at risk if you are touching metal, and especially if you are bridging two metal components—the wheel and a stanchion, for example. And if the mast is poorly grounded, *side flashes*—a leap from the mast to other parts of the boat—can also cause injury. Even with a good ground, it is wise to stay well away from the mast during an electrical storm.

WOODEN MASTS

IF YOUR BOAT has a wooden mast, you need a metal lightning rod extending above everything at the masthead by at least 6 inches (15 cm) and connected to ground with #4 AWG wire. Without the metal rod, wooden masts struck by lightning tend to blow apart as the high resistance generates enough heat to instantly convert moisture in the wood to steam. A pointed dissipator, called an *air terminal*, makes a fine lightning rod.

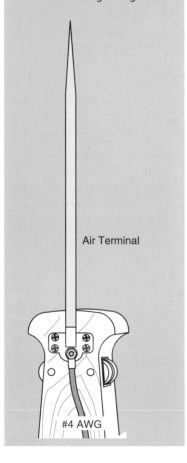

Air Terminal

#4 AWG

GROUND

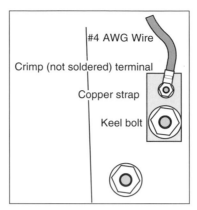

#4 AWG Wire

Crimp (not soldered) terminal

Copper strap

Keel bolt

A metal keel makes an excellent ground for a lightning protection system. Bottom paint does not act as a significant barrier to a strike that has gotten this far in its quest to reach the water.

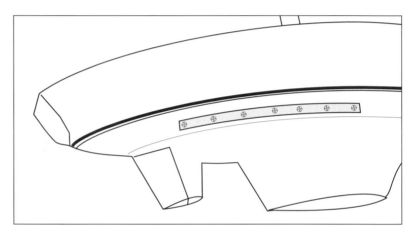

If your keel is encapsulated, a copper ground plate is needed. Lightning dissipates from the edge of the plate, so the perimeter of the plate should be at least 4 feet (1.2 m) if you sail in salt water. If there is any chance that you might sail in freshwater, the ground plate should have at least 24 feet (7.3 m) of sharp edge, usually accomplished by attaching a 12-foot (3.7 m) length of 1-inch (2.5 cm) copper strap fore and aft. Bronze bolts are preferred over stainless steel for bolting the plate to the hull and for cable attachment.

Sintered bronze plates designed for grounding radios are a poor choice for conducting lightning to ground. They are less effective than solid copper at dissipating the charge of a strike, and reportedly they tend to explode when heat from the strike turns trapped water to steam.

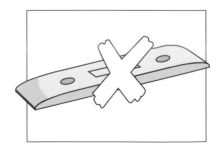

Do not route the strike through the engine. The propeller might have enough edge length to do the job in salt water, but passing such high voltage through the engine can damage the bearings. Likewise, never ground the mast to a sea cock. The lack of adequate conductivity is almost certain to generate enough heat to melt the fitting right out of the hull. And then where are you?

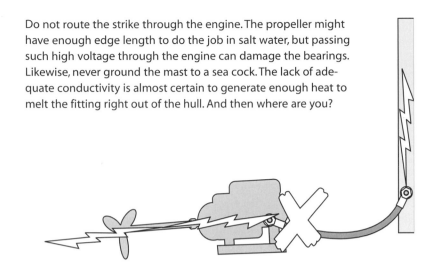

DIRECTING THE CHARGE

Connect the mast to the underwater ground with #4 AWG or larger cable. Because lightning travels on the surface of the conductor, solid copper strap is an even better choice. I like $^1/_2$-inch copper tubing (water pipe), first radiused then flattened.

Lightning doesn't like to change direction, so conductors should lead as straight as possible to the ground. If a turn is required, give it a radius of 12 inches (30 cm) or more. Even if your mast sits directly on the keel, perfect the electrical connection with a copper strap from the mast to a keel bolt.

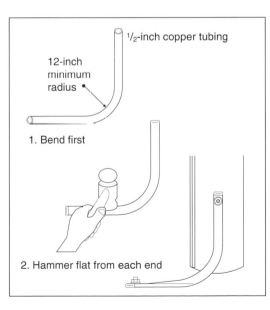

$^1/_2$-inch copper tubing

12-inch minimum radius

1. Bend first

2. Hammer flat from each end

CONNECTIONS

The electrical connections must be perfect. The current flow in a lightning strike ranges from around 20,000 to nearly 400,000 amps, so a 1-ohm resistance can cause a 400,000-volt difference (I x R) from one side of the connection to the other. The result is enough heat to vaporize metal, and the resistance may encourage dangerous side flashes.

Drill attachment holes in the ends of copper strap. Cable connections should be made with mechanically attached terminals—solder will melt. Be sure all connections are clean and tight, and use copper washers to increase the contact area—except use stainless steel washers on the mast connection to minimize corrosion. Coat the assembled connection with an anti-corrosion spray, and disassemble and clean it at least once a year to make sure it stays resistance-free. Periodically check the resistance from the mast to the ground plate with your ohmmeter.

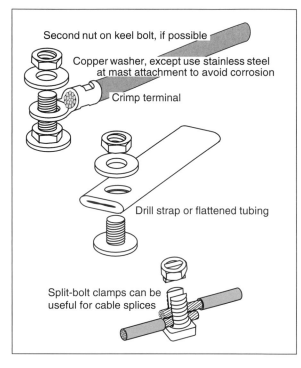

Second nut on keel bolt, if possible

Copper washer, except use stainless steel at mast attachment to avoid corrosion

Crimp terminal

Drill strap or flattened tubing

Split-bolt clamps can be useful for cable splices

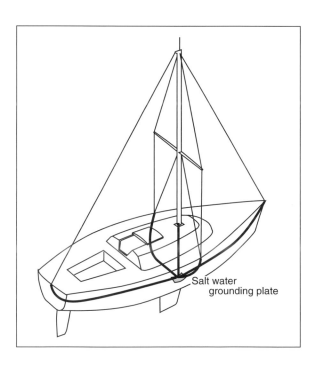

Salt water grounding plate

PARALLEL PATHS

Although an aluminum mast offers lower resistance than steel stays, a powerful strike may nevertheless induce current flow in stays and shrouds. To provide this current a safe path to ground, the chainplates should also be connected to the underwater ground. Here again, the route should be as direct as possible with only large radius changes of direction. You can use #6 AWG for these secondary grounding paths.

BONDING

The original idea behind bonding was to put all underwater fittings at the same potential to stop galvanic corrosion. Unfortunately, this type of bonding invites more-destructive stray-current corrosion. Bonding is still intended to put fittings at the same potential, but today the purpose is to prevent side flashes from voltage differences in the event of a lightning strike.

The rules for bonding are simple: bond all sizable metal components within 6 feet (1.8 m) of the mast or rigging to the mast ground, but do not bond any submerged metal (ground plate excepted).

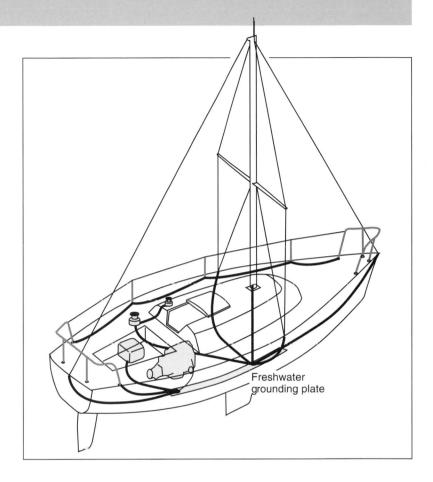

Freshwater grounding plate

FOR LIGHTNING PROTECTION

During a lightning strike, when the mast has a potential of 30,000 volts and other metal components inside the boat are essentially at 0 volts, there is some risk of the lightning jumping to the lower potential. This is called a *side flash* and it is extremely dangerous to anyone in its path. To minimize this risk, give the charge a lower-resistance path by connecting all significant metal masses (e.g., tanks, stove, lifelines) within 6 feet (1.8 m) of the mast or rigging to the ground plate. Use #6 AWG wire (or larger), and connect each component to the ground with a dedicated wire.

FOR CORROSION CONTROL

If underwater components are not galvanically identical, bonding them completes the circuit and *causes* corrosion (which must be controlled with zinc anodes). Bonding does protect underwater fittings from damage caused by onboard stray currents, but it invites damage from stray currents in the water, and "hot" marinas are today the rule rather than the exception. It is easy enough to avoid onboard stray currents with good wiring practices, but you have no control over stray currents in the water. *No good can come from bonding underwater metal components that are or could be otherwise isolated.*

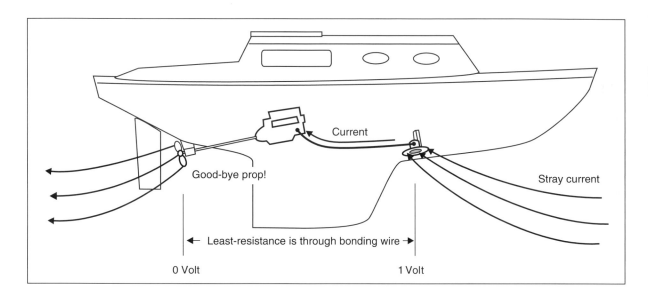

ISOLATING

Metal through-hulls connected to rubber hose are already isolated. Likewise, the rudder shaft and/or fittings are normally isolated, but be sure components are not grounded some other way. For example, the rudder might be connected to the boat's central ground through steering cables and pedestal wiring. A fuel tank connected to the engine with metal fuel line is likewise electrically connected to the DC ground. In this latter case, bonding the tank for lightning protection provides a path for stray current to enter your boat at the ground plate and pass out at the prop (or vice versa).

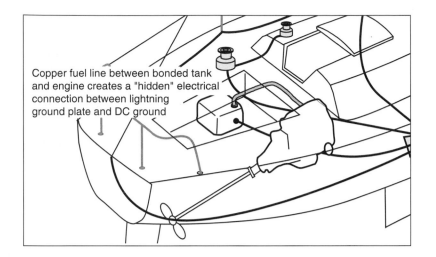

Copper fuel line between bonded tank and engine creates a "hidden" electrical connection between lightning ground plate and DC ground

Isolate bonded tanks by inserting a section of rubber hose in the fuel line. The propeller and shaft are easily isolated with a flexible coupling. (Note: A zinc collar is still required to protect the bronze prop if the shaft is steel.)

GROUNDING

The general rule for corrosion control is to bond to a single underwater component. This eliminates any possibility of providing a circuit for stray current, and it also eliminates galvanic currents except between dissimilar metals in contact. The preferred configuration is to isolate the propeller shaft from the engine so the prop doesn't provide a ground, then use the lightning grounding plate for all ground connections. If the engine is not isolated, the necessity for ground near the base of the mast means you will have two bonded components in the water. Copper and bronze are close enough on the galvanic scale that significant galvanic corrosion is not likely, but stray current corrosion is a risk. The solution in this case is to keep the lightning ground electrically separated from the engine ground (for the DC and AC circuits).

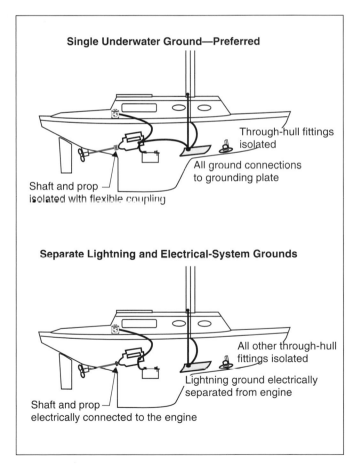

Single Underwater Ground—Preferred

Through-hull fittings isolated

All ground connections to grounding plate

Shaft and prop isolated with flexible coupling

Separate Lightning and Electrical-System Grounds

All other through-hull fittings isolated

Lightning ground electrically separated from engine

Shaft and prop electrically connected to the engine

TESTING FOR ISOLATION

Measure the resistance between the lightning ground terminal and the DC ground terminal. In salt water the meter should read around 200 kΩ per foot of underwater separation between the ground plate and the stern tube, about 2 MΩ per foot in freshwater. A low resistance reading reveals a connection between the two grounds. Disconnect one bonding cable at a time until the meter reading changes: the unwanted connection is through the just-disconnected component.

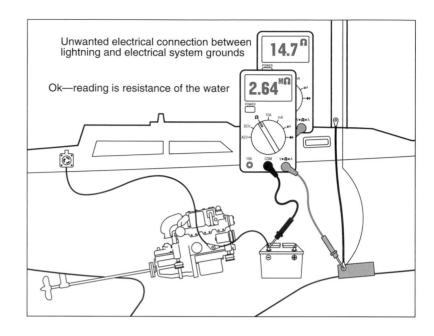

Unwanted electrical connection between lightning and electrical system grounds

Ok—reading is resistance of the water

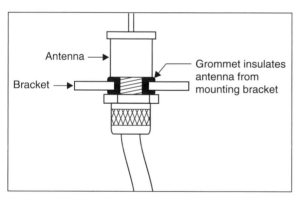

Antenna →

Bracket →

Grommet insulates antenna from mounting bracket

Often you will find that the connection is through the mast, usually due to contact between a masthead antenna bracket and the coax shield. You can break this connection by installing insulating grommets around the bracket mounting bolts or in the antenna-mount hole.

Radio equipment may also be grounded to the engine and other metal components in the boat. If it is also connected to the lightning ground plate—as it should be—this is another electrical connection between the lightning ground and the DC ground. We deal with this problem below.

RF GROUND

SB and ham radios need a good ground to provide the necessary counterpoise for transmission—like planting your feet to jump or throw. A good radio ground is a large mass of metal very close to but not necessarily touching seawater. This is usually accommodated by grounding the radio to the engine, other large metal components, and to the water through a ground plate. The lightning ground plate serves well.

RIBBON, NOT WIRE

Radio grounds should be made with copper foil ribbon, not wire, because the current we want the conductor to carry is RF (radio frequency), not DC. RF currents travel on the surface of the conductor (lightning is also an RF event), so the more surface, the less the conductor impedes the RF current. This essentially means less of your radio's power is wasted in the ground system, so more is radiated from your antenna. That translates into longer range and clearer signals.

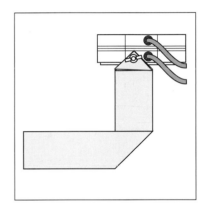

Use 3-inch-wide (7.6 cm) foil ribbon for the best RF ground connection. Fold the ends into a point for terminal attachment. Bend the foil around corners and obstacles as shown.

COPPER SCREEN

Today's automatic antenna tuners compensate for a less-than-perfect counterpoise, so few boats bother with "building" a counterpoise, relying instead on the metal masses already in the boat combined with a good "connection" to the ocean. Still, for the best radio installation, about 100 square feet (9.3 m²) of copper screening inside the hull can avoid a lot of transmission problems. Hardware stores sell copper screening for windows inexpensively, and it is easy to install in below-the-waterline lockers, covered with a layer of lightweight fiberglass cloth. However, because the wire in the screening is just woven together, corrosion may eventually degrade their electrical contact. Soldering two edges before installation avoids this problem. Join the various screen panels with 3-inch (7.6 cm) foil tape, also soldered.

STOPPING DIRECT CURRENT

Not only does the RF ground system not need to carry DC, but we don't want it to because that allows the flow of destructive stray current. This is easily prevented by cutting the foil ribbon leading to the ground plate and installing the ends on a double bus circuit block, leaving a gap of about $^1/_{16}$ inch. Now bridge the gap with a 0.15μF ceramic capacitor (available for under a buck from most electronics suppliers). You can solder the capacitor to the ribbon, or if the leads are long enough, simply capture them under an opposing pair of the terminal screws. The capacitor passes RF current but blocks DC.

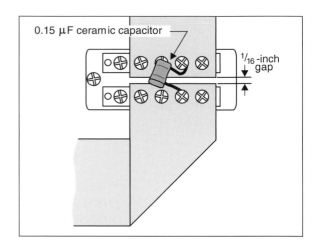

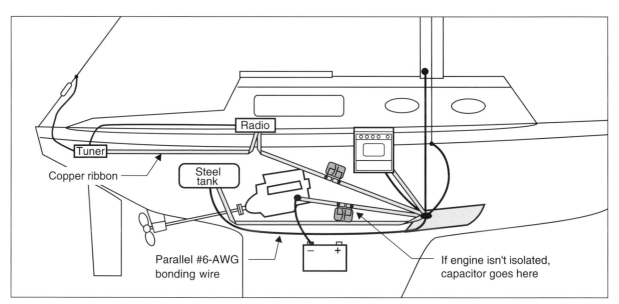

If other metal components bonded for lightning protection are also connected to the RF ground system, disconnect RF connections from the components to the radio and make them to the ground plate. Configured this way, a single capacitor will separate the DC ground from the RF ground. If your foil is thick enough—at least 9 mils (0.009 inches)—you can substitute the ribbon for the wire; otherwise connect the ribbon parallel to the #6 AWG bonding wire.

LIGHTNING AND ELECTRONICS

While a lightning-protection system can nearly eliminate personal risk and significantly reduce damage to the boat, it offers little if any protection for electronics. About half the boats struck by lightning experience damage to some or all of the electronics aboard.

THE FACTS

Like any moving current, lightning can induce current to flow in any conductor it passes near. Considering the enormous power of lightning, "near" might well be 100 yards or more. The closer and more powerful the strike, the more current that is induced. Such currents often exceed the capacity of the tiny, low-current components inside most electronics. Since electronics need not be connected to anything to be affected, disconnecting them does not prevent damage.

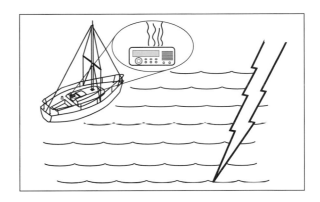

PROTECTIVE MEASURES

A surge protector in the supply line may provide protection for a limited range of lightning-induced power spikes. Twist all electronics power leads so induced currents will tend to cancel. All bonding wires should cross electrical wiring at 90 degrees to minimize the inductive effect of current flowing to ground. Grounding the chassis—the metal housing—protects internal circuits and components from directly induced currents. But despite every protective effort, if your boat is struck, your electronics have only one chance in two of not becoming toast. So the best protective measure is keeping your insurance paid up.

INDEX

DON CASEY credits the around-the-world voyage of Robin Lee Graham, featured in *National Geographic* in the late 1960s, with opening his eyes to the world beyond the shoreline. After graduating from the University of Texas he moved to south Florida, where he began to spend virtually all his leisure time messing about in boats.

In 1983 he abandoned a career in banking to devote more time to cruising and writing. His work combining these two passions soon began to appear in many popular sailing and boating magazines. In 1986 he co-authored *Sensible Cruising: The Thoreau Approach*, an immediate best-seller and the book responsible for pushing many would-be cruisers over the horizon. He is also author of *This Old Boat*, a universally praised guide that has led thousands of boatowners through the process of turning a rundown production boat into a first-class yacht, and of *Sailboat Refinishing*, *Sailboat Hull & Deck Repair*, *Canvaswork & Sail Repair*, and *Inspecting the Aging Sailboat*, all part of the International Marine Sailboat Library. He continues to evaluate old and new products and methods, often trying them on his own 30-year-old, much-modified, Allied Seawind.

When not writing or off cruising, he can be found sailing on Florida's Biscayne Bay.

THE INTERNATIONAL MARINE SAILBOAT LIBRARY

Sailboat Electrics Simplified has company:

Sailboat Refinishing
by Don Casey
Hardcover, 144 pages, 350 illustrations, $21.95. Item No. 013225-9

Sailboat Hull & Deck Repair
by Don Casey
Hardcover, 144 pages, 350 illustrations, $21.95. Item No. 013369-7

Canvaswork & Sail Repair
by Don Casey
Hardcover, 144 pages, 350 illustrations, $21.95. Item No. 013391-3

The Sailor's Assistant:
Reference Data for Maintenance, Repair, & Cruising
by John Vigor
Hardcover, 176 pages, 140 illustrations, $21.95. Item No. 067476-0

Troubleshooting Marine Diesels
by Peter Compton
Hardcover, 176 pages, 200 illustrations, $21.95. Item No. 012354-3

Inspecting the Aging Sailboat
by Don Casey
Hardcover, 144 pages, 300 illustrations, $21.95. Item No. 013394-8

100 Fast and Easy Boat Improvements
by Don Casey
Hardcover, 144 pages, 200 illustrations, $21.95. Item No. 013402-2

Boatowner's Weekend Woodworking
by Garth Graves
Hardcover, 144 pages, 200 illustrations, $21.95. Item No. 024696-3